The
Coronation
of Love

The Coronation of Love

A MEMOIR

Losing, Seeking, & Finding the Greatest Gift of All

STEPHANIE MURRAY

ILLUMIFY
MEDIA.COM

The Coronation of Love

Copyright © 2024 by Stephanie Murray

Published by

Illumify Media Global

www.IllumifyMedia.com

"Let's bring your book to life!"

Paperback ISBN: 978-1-964251-00-4

Cover design by Debbie Lewis

Photograph by Corey Myers

Printed in the United States of America

This book is dedicated to my heavenly Father and Friend, Jesus Christ, who called me to tell our story.

To my parents and brothers: our home was the first place I witnessed and experienced unconditional love.

To my children, Eli'el and Kadiri: both of you are the reason I sought to find love.

To anyone who searched for love and didn't know who or what it was, this book is for you.

Contents

Part Five: Finding Love

PART 1

LOVE'S FOUNDATION

1

Identifying Love

"*STEPHANIE* MEANS CROWN," MY brother Jonathan explained to me at a family meeting one Sunday afternoon at my grandma Murray's house. He had looked up the meaning of the names of every individual in our immediate family, as well as our cousin Celeste.

Jonathan went on to say, "If we possess a greater understanding of who we are, I'm hoping this knowledge will propel us to become who *God* created us to be and not merely the person *we* have created ourselves to be from our brokenness."

He looked directly at me. "Stephanie, as you know, a crown is a circular ornamental headdress worn by a monarch as a symbol of authority, usually made of or decorated with precious metals and jewels. But there are a few things you might not know. A crown is a symbol of honor and authority for monarchs."

I listened intently. When I was a child, my mother created a framed keepsake listing the names of all the children in our family, along with their meaning. I had always known my name meant *crown*, but Jonathan was sharing with me a number of things I had never known.

"A crown is also the top of a steeple, or the highest point of something; the turning apparatus used to set a clock; the upper part of a cut gem; or the point of an anchor at which the arms reach the shaft," Jonathan continued. "In other words, Stephanie, you are supposed to reach great heights in life because the distance you go gives others around you permission to do the same."

It was a moving and intimate time with our family as Jonathan spoke empowering words to each of us about our names. We all came away that day with a deeper, fuller reverence of our identity and calling.

Like me, you are also called by name and throughout our lives our identities are discovered. 1 Peter 2:9 says we were called to be "a chosen generation, a royal priesthood, a holy nation, His own special people, that you may proclaim the praises of Him who called you out of darkness into His marvelous light." Who we are at our core will one day be revealed. In that moment, we must make a choice to either embrace the truth or turn away from the truth and embrace a lie.

Pondering Jonathan's words made me realize I had a more significant part to play in my life and in the lives of all those connected to me. Suddenly, I was aware of a new identity, yet I wasn't ready to answer the call: the call to believe in myself and be all of who I was created to be. My longing for love distracted me from realizing my true identity.

Regretfully, in the moment when I should have been fully present and open to receive the blessing and fullness of my name, I was distracted. Plans to meet up with my boyfriend had me preoccupied while my brother shared his God-given insights. I felt anxious about running late and disappointing my boyfriend. Early in our relationship, I discovered that small things easily became huge misunderstandings. Often, he accused me of caring more about family than him.

I knew his behavior was unreasonable, yet instead of identifying it as a red flag, I hung on to the belief that our love would overcome our challenges. I prematurely put the expectations of a marriage relationship on an immature, non-covenantal relationship.

I should have known better.

After all, I'd seen a beautiful role model of covenantal love exemplified in the union of my parents, Eric and Risa Murray. My parents' relationship with God and with each other provided a solid foundation for the family they'd created. Through their example, I came to believe that real love fostered hope, commitment, and sacrifice—during the good and bad times.

Their marriage wasn't perfect. What marriage is? During their journey together, they first discovered God's love. Then they were able to love themselves and develop a Christ-centered love for one another and their community.

First Generation

My parents' love story began when they met at church in a group of friends. They became first-generation Pentecostals in the eighties where friendship and curiosity prompted their journey in discovering a love for God, for themselves, and for one another.

My dad explained his conversion experience to me: "A friend of mine went to church and began teaching Bible study classes. Out of curiosity, I flipped through one of her Bible study charts. Soon after, I began attending her church and agreed to go to one of her Bible study classes. After completing the Bible study, I felt like something had changed within me, and I decided to get baptized.

"Before I got baptized, I was so angry. I lived with what felt like a ball in the pit of my stomach every day. After I was baptized, the ball in my stomach immediately melted away. I got out of the water and was filled with so much love and joy. I remember hugging everyone I could! Prior to my act of faith in baptism, I was hurt and closed off I would've never done that."

My mom's experience was similar. One day, Valerie, her old college roommate, greeted her with the words, "Praise the Lord, Risa!" My mom couldn't have been more shocked! After all, my mom knew Valerie prior, and neither of them had been particularly religious. Sometimes they hung out and smoked weed together! The change in Valerie was evidence to my mom that something significant had happened, and she wanted to learn more.

"I was searching for God, and it sounded like my friend was on a similar path and had discovered a new life," Mom explained. "I began going to church with Valerie. One evening, I was baptized in someone's tub at a home fellowship and received the infilling of the Holy Spirit. I experienced immense joy when I entered into a relationship with Jesus."

Although my parents grew up in the same neighborhood and went to the same school—my dad even knew my mom's brother!—they never met until they were both in church. They began their journey by first coming to love God and they believed they loved one another. On December 6, 1986, they got married.

I love looking at my parents' wedding photos. My mom was beautiful with baby's breath placed throughout her curls, and my dad's smile was the biggest and brightest I've ever seen. Surrounded by their families, childhood friends, and church parishioners, they were married during the weekly Sunday morning church service. Throngs of people were there in support and celebration of their union.

My parents shared with me how all their family and friends came together to decorate, prepare food, sing, and offer their help. Through the pictures, I experienced the smiles, outfits, food, wedding party, and festivities. My mom's cousins sang, and an epic potluck-style reception followed the ceremony.

As a child, I decided I wanted to marry and become a beautiful bride like my mom. I'd hoped my future husband would smile as brightly as my dad did on his wedding day. I remember being excited at the thought that I'd have a family of my own, filled with children and laughter.

As an adult, I interviewed my parents about their commitment to their marriage of over thirty years. My parents dated briefly and undoubtedly needed more time to get to know one another. They never attended premarital counseling, which they both say was unwise. Perhaps if they went to counseling, they would have discovered how to become honest, transparent, and vulnerable with one another. Unfortunately, they didn't know what they didn't know until they were in crisis.

Soon after they were married, they experienced multiple changes within the first year that destabilized them as individuals and as a couple. For example, my dad took a job in another city, which caused them to move away from family and friends. Two months into their marriage, they became pregnant with me. Before long, they realized their expectations of one another weren't being communicated and were therefore unmet. Sadly, they struggled to connect.

Multiple changes and stressors are difficult to navigate, especially with a lack of community, counseling, and guidance from older couples or family members, or even friendships offering accountability. It's difficult to know what to prioritize in an uncharted relationship, yet they did the only thing they knew to do.

In the thick of their trial, my mom heard a Christian broadcast called *Focus on the Family*. She then bought the cassette tape box set, and they both listened to it together. While they listened, the speakers gave them words for what they were experiencing. They no longer felt alone and could finally begin to understand and navigate through all the simultaneous changes they'd encountered within their first year of marriage.

I've been graced to have had countless enlightening and honest conversations with my parents as an adult. Unfortunately, I realized that my parents went through many challenging times as a married couple alone. Even when they were together as a nucleus, they were still alone. Very rarely did they have the benefit of having godly counsel, account-ability, or mentorship as individuals or as a couple. My parents kept trying; they didn't leave or give up when it was difficult.

There were times that God sent help to my parents in the gift of loving relationships.

My dad recalled a story where he was running to the bus stop and heard a woman shouting to him from her porch: Mrs. Jackson.

"Are you a Christian?" she called out.

"Yes!" he yelled back as he ran to catch his bus to work.

Later in the day, he was walking home and the same woman was on her porch. She invited my mom and him over for a spaghetti dinner and to watch a video. My dad thought it was strange; however, he has always been an inquisitive man, so he came along with my mom.

When they arrived at Mrs. Jackson's home, she made their plates and then showed them a video of her daughters' wedding. Both my parent's cried when they witnessed the love shown.

Mrs. Jackson and her family were gifts from God to my parents. My dad referred to Mrs. Jackson as "raw, yet honest and loving." She was a phenomenal teacher who lived a life of loving and teaching all those who would receive her words. She and her husband, along with their daughters, sons,

sons-in-law, and grandchildren, wanted people to live loving, abundant, purposeful lives.

My parents received help and guidance from the Jackson family as far as my parents allowed them, which wasn't fully. Their lack of trust and fear prevented them from fully receiving the gifts God sent them in the form of people. At the time, my parents had been so hurt and endured so much pain, they didn't know how to let people in. The pain they carried from their past, compounded by the challenges of the present, eventually became problematic.

Whether the struggle was a lack of trust in themselves or one another, financial hardships, feelings of inadequacy, married life, parenthood, work, and even the church, they chose to stay committed.

Regardless of their frailties, God covered them in grace and mercy because they didn't know better. Thankfully, over the years my parents have grown by leaps and bounds as they have gotten older and overcame major opposition. The greatest lesson my parents taught me was love is marked by commitment and faithfulness, forged in difficult times. I didn't realize it then; however, I identified the foundation of love as commitment to God, to family, to oneself, and to neighbors through giving relationships.

A Namesake

My parents often told my siblings and me the story of when they decided on how many children they wanted to have. Before my parents married, they rode the bus to church together. While riding, they discussed different topics. One ride my parents asked one another, "How many children do you want to have?"

They always laughed when they told the next part of the story, exclaiming to us proudly, "We decided on a half dozen!"

Everyone has plans until experience sets in, and the same was true of my parents. After my mom gave birth to their fifth child, she decided she was liable to die if she gave birth again, so she and my dad decided to "close up shop" as they call it. Although my parents planned to have a family and were excited about having children, I was conceived a lot earlier than either of them expected.

"Your dad and I went to a restaurant, and afterward I felt extremely sick," my mom recalled. "'Something is wrong, I need to go to hospital,' I told your dad. When we got there, the doctor asked if there was a possibility I could be pregnant. I looked at him and said, 'Well, yeah!'"

Doctors told my parents they were having a boy, so they chose the name Stephen after Stephen in the Bible. Then, because God has a sense of humor, my mom gave birth to me, their one and only daughter, on October 7. As soon as my parents welcomed me, they changed my name to Stephanie, the female version of Stephen, at the suggestion of Aunt Crandallyn. This began a tradition. My parents named all four of my brothers and me after men in the Bible.

So why Stephen? What was it my parents admired in his character that caused them to name their firstborn after him? Stephen was first mentioned in Acts 6 when he was described as a man who was "full of faith and the Holy Spirit" (v. 5). Apostles appointed Stephen to help the widows in Greece. He was chosen because he was an honest believer and follower of Jesus. Stephen was described as ministering in wisdom and performing great wonders and miracles among the people as he shared the truth about Jesus. Stephen was so bold and effective, the religious people began to dispute with him until they arrested him for speaking against God!

Truly, he spoke against their lack of love for God and people. After he told his nation the truth, Acts 7:54 says, "they were cut to the heart" and were so enraged they threw him out of the city.

The account of Stephen's death is in Acts 7:59–60: "And they stoned Stephen as he was calling on God and saying, 'Lord Jesus, receive my spirit.' Then he knelt down and cried out with a loud voice, 'Lord, do not charge them with this sin.' And when he had said this, he fell asleep."

Even up to his death, Stephen maintained the courage to speak the truth, forgive, and cry out in compassion for the people of his nation, regardless of them being his enemies and stoning him. His love was extraordinarily. I was twenty-seven years old before I realized that the love Stephen displayed was supernatural, and pure the evidence of someone who was filled with the Spirit of God.

Although I was unable to articulate what love was until I was twenty-five, I was able to identify what love was not because I experienced love from my parents, my family, and my community as a child. Love in its purest form is supernatural. This is the journey that lead me to knowing this truth.

2

Modeling Love

MY GRANDMOTHER LIVED IN a small two-bedroom house in Denver's Five Points neighborhood. Despite its diminutive size, her home always served as a gathering place for the family. Sunday afternoons, our entire family—including aunts, uncles, and cousins—would eat dinner at my grandparents' house. Some of my fondest memories were of my cousin's Marti, Shelli and Kelli laughing from their souls. Or my Uncles Leonard and Chucky's good natured humor. My aunt Linda had a kind demeanor and my uncle Harold and aunt Karen displayed the spirit of hospitality. I can still sense the increase of love I felt from each embrace I had from all of my younger cousins as they were born and grew up along side me. Grandma Murray would cook fried chicken, greens, rice, cornbread, and gravy and sometimes she'd even make a roast with potatoes and carrots.

One of my earliest memories was watching Grandma and Grandpa Murray wash dishes after a Sunday dinner. I was as tall as their kneecaps and remember tilting my head all the way back in order to see their faces.

As dinner was being prepared, my cousins would watch basketball. One Sunday, I stood in front of the tiny box TV and asked my older cousins, "Where is Michael Jordan?"

They tilted their heads around me and said, "Sit down. Just look for number twenty-three!" I attempted to follow the game and their excitement as they followed Jordan's every move.

While my older cousins watched TV, my educator aunts and uncles would always ask me about school or my friends.

Grandma Murray

Grandma Murray was a friendly person. Her face would light up when she saw me. I would go on trips with her to the bank or shopping. My first airplane trip was with her to attend my cousin Marti's wedding in California. Every time we would go downtown on the train, we went to Taco Bell.

On our trips we would talk.

Grandma Murray purchased two houses on the same block. When she told me what she'd paid for them, she was so proud. "You know how much I paid for this house?" She'd pause as if to give me a chance to guess before excitedly telling me, "Five thousand dollars! Do you know how much I paid for the second house?" She paused for effect again. "Ten thousand dollars!" My eyes widened. She beamed as I smiled back at her.

My grandma was a smart, hardworking, giving, kind-hearted woman who loved people, especially her family. I felt safe at my grandma's house because she was there. Her biggest teaching is what she modeled for me: love is kind.

When I was almost two and a half, my brother Jonathan was born. Within that same year, my parents fell on hard times, and we moved in with Grandma Murray for a while. While we were living at her house, my second brother, Andrew, was born.

I was four and remember my excitement as my mom came up the steps to my grandmother's house, cradling the newest edition to our family. My dad and mom set up a crib in the living room. Since the crib was close to the floor, I often stood on my tippy toes and peered over the railing to see Andrew. Peering through the slats didn't give me a good enough view, so I learned how to pull my body up so I could see over the edge.

Shortly after Andrew was born, my mom was back in the hospital, but I didn't know why. I stayed with Grandma Murray during the day, which was fine, yet I remember missing my mom. At my young age, I didn't have words for what my mom was experiencing. Now I know she was struggling with postpartum depression.

After she was in the hospital a few days, I talked to her on the phone.

"How old are you?" she asked.

How could she not know my age? I looked at the phone and began to cry in confusion. *Why is my mom in the hospital? Is she sick? When is she going to come back?* I felt unsettled without her presence.

After some time, my mom came back and I felt better. I would walk beside her as she pushed my younger brothers in a double stroller around the city. We'd go to doctor appointments or the grocery store. I stayed close and helped her out with my brothers.

Recently, my mom shared with me some of the support she received during this time. While my mom was in the hospital, her sisters, Collette and Kathy, came and prayed with her. "At a time when I felt the most lost and afraid, my sisters came to pray with me. Your Aunt Kathy also bought me a paint set and left it with me in the hospital. I hadn't done art in many years; however, art helped me find joy again. I needed a creative outlet. Women from our church would also come and sit with me during the day and share their testimonies. I even began going to Ladies Fitness to work out."

A Secret

After my parents got back on their feet financially, we moved into a house of our own. My mother was feeling better by then, and my parents felt hopeful everything would turn out okay. They enrolled me in preschool, and my mom walked me to school and back every day. She often visited with the other moms. One day, my mom and I visited the home of one of my classmates. After we all had a snack, our mothers chatted at the kitchen table while my friend and I went off to play. We ran together up a long staircase to get to her room.

After playing with a lot of her toys, she asked, "Want to go into my closet? I want to show you something."

She introduced me to a game called House, in which children pretend and take on the roles and behaviors of adults. This game gave me a strange but exhilarating feeling. Although I don't recall her telling me to keep it a secret, the act felt secretive. Because we weren't in her room; instead, we were hiding in her closet. This is the first secret I ever had. After our visit, I went home with my mom, and thankfully we never visited their home again.

My classmate molested me. The game I was taught and the feelings it evoked stayed with me and brought trouble into my life for many years to come. Several years later my God dad had a conversation with my dad that my dad shared with me. My God dad said when perversion enters a child's life, they either perpetuate the same actions or become a participant in other perverse activities. Sadly, this is what happened to me and so many others.

Our Home

When I turned five, my family moved to apartment 202 in the suburbs. Both my parents were raised in Colorado, even though both of their families were from the South. My parents grew up in Denver and began raising us there. After I finished Head Start, my parents moved us all to Thornton in hopes we would receive a better education.

Our three-bedroom apartment had a small kitchen, living room, dining room, linen closet, and a coat closet my mom turned into her art studio. At times, I enjoyed having my own room. Other times, I shared a room with one or two of my brothers. We got used to sharing and being in close proximity in the apartment.

Growing up, I would describe my mom as creative, hard-working, and introspective. She taught my brothers and me everything. First on her list was how to clean. We learned how to clean our rooms, then she taught us how to clean the kitchen and bathroom. We were taught how to sweep and mop as well as how to wash and dry our own clothes. She taught us how to wash up and the importance of deodorant. She embraced quite a task making sure all of us wore clean clothes, brushed our teeth, washed our faces, and combed our hair. My mom also taught us Bible verses and the Ten Commandments.

When we were young, she read books to us almost every night. As we got older, she read novels to us. For years, she was our Sunday school teacher too.

My mom was very talented with her hands and enjoyed making puppets and various crafts. She introduced my brothers and me to her love of art through painting. One of her best skills was cooking. Personally, I loved baking cookies with her during the holidays the most. Whenever it was our birthday, my mom would cook a spread.

Something significant about my mom was that when I was younger, she didn't chitchat. Our conversations were task-oriented and revolved around learning. I truly felt that her main objective was for us to be responsible and to behave.

Yet . . . my mom would not have been the woman she was without *her* mother.

When we visited Grandma LaVonne, I understood my mom better. Grandma LaVonne was orderly; her home was organized and neat. No one wondered where they stood with her. If you were doing anything you shouldn't be doing she would correct you. Her expectations were clear. She always wore peep-toe shoes and dressed sharp and trendy.

Always a present figure in my life, she and my Grandma Murray came to my school for Grandparent's Day. In middle school, she was there to celebrate my induction into the National Honors Society. One year, my cousins and I went with her to Take Your Child to Work Day before she retired from the state. Grandma LaVonne was an excellent cook, serving and supporting our family any way she could. I have fond memories of watching my uncle Jody and aunt Felicia or my aunts Kathy and Collette host cookouts. A melody of laughter surrounded the card tables. My older cousins Tywanda and Tiffany laughed so hard I had to at least smile. All my younger cousins played as earnestly as they could without crossing the bondaries in whatever home we were visiting. I got to know her better as I got older. The same was true of my mom; I knew her once I became a young woman and a mother. They both taught me love never fails.

On the other hand, my dad was a dynamic communicator. He was charismatic, funny, kind, and a dreamer. He was easier to connect with because he liked to talk. Pretending I was sleeping in the car so my dad would carry me up the stairs to our apartment became a regular occurrence. He was my hero—the tallest, the strongest, and the best man in my world.

Often, I would see my dad drinking hot tea, reading the newspaper, and laughing at the comics in the back. Other times we would just sit around, talking and eating. My dad would carry my brothers, Jonathan and Andrew, on his back like a horse as he crawled across the living room floor. When he was present, it was usually for a short time before my brothers and I would head to school or go to bed. He worked hard all the time. For most my life, he worked nights. Unfortunately, his work schedule made it near impossible to have consistent, meaningful connections. Life seemed to be better when he was present for all of us.

Otherwise, we shared our time with Dad with members of the church we went to. We saw him teaching the congregation, praying, or serving others. My dad was liked by most his peers, yet he was only close to a few people. Whenever I had a need, I asked my dad. I knew we didn't have much, yet I knew if my dad could give us something we needed or wanted, he would.

At home, my parents never cursed. If my brothers or I cursed or lied, our mouths were washed out with soap. Sometimes we were spanked. I know these practices are frowned upon today; however, back then they were less taboo. Rarely would my parents correct me in anger. There were times my mom got angry and she'd yell, yet it was never obscenities.

With three kids who often didn't listen and occasionally pressed the boundaries, I'm sure it was overwhelming for her. Even though those weren't the best interactions, I could tell the difference between how I heard other parents talk to their children while I played outside and how my parents interacted with my brothers and me.

Another thing I observed in apartment 202 was how my parents interacted. I watched them like a movie, moving my head back and forth as they talked. Without knowing it, I was attempting to grasp what I could about marriage through their relationship.

We didn't hear a lot of arguing or big disagreements between them in those days. I never heard my parents demean each other. At times, my parents talked in the car and spelled out words before I could read because I was a nosey child.

My dad would often wash the dishes after my mom cooked dinner. Sometimes my dad would get home and bring my mom flowers or other small gifts. My parents always gave each other cards, and at times they would go to marriage retreats and celebrate anniversaries together. These interactions increased my desire to be married and have a family when I got older.

During my childhood, my parents didn't own a television. My brothers, cousins, Jinnelle and Celeste, and I made up games and played outside all the time, even during the winter. I loved playing bank. My role was banker, and my brothers were my wealthy clients. We built forts and tents and pretended we were Indians, like Hiawatha. We were inspired to be like him after seeing the film countless times at Grandma LaVonne's house.

When we got a little older, we were allowed to explore more on our own. My mom grew up in the country in Colorado. Her experience caused her to allow us to explore like she and her siblings did. We caught crawdads, frogs, and minnows in the pond and ditch next to our apartment. We listened to interesting, funny, and dramatic stories on the radio. Our favorite program was *Adventures in Odyssey*.

Often, our cousins would spend the night and play Monopoly or cards. For quite a while a prank war began that consisted mostly of placing raw eggs in one another's beds. In the summer, we rode bikes and walked to the neighborhood store by ourselves to buy a snack. The trips to the store felt liberating at first until the store attendant consistently followed us around to ensure we weren't stealing anything.

What the store attendant didn't know was that we were terrified to steal because my parents discussed the consequences of stealing with us in our family meetings. In these family meetings, my parents read devotionals that taught life lessons. We also heard personal stories from Mom and Dad. One time, my mom told us a story of when she stole things from the store.

"The security guard said, 'You're going to jail!'" Mom said. "I cried and cried."

My brothers and I listened to my mom's tales, wide-eyed. I decided then I wouldn't steal anything from the store.

The most impactful lesson my dad taught me was not to mistreat people, especially my brothers. Physically hitting or hurting one another was unacceptable. One year, we were on our way to church camp when Jonathan and I got into an argument and began hitting each other. My dad spanked both of us. Needless to say, we never hit one another again.

Whenever we would argue and my dad was within earshot, he would quickly correct us. I'm so thankful Dad taught us to treat one another well. He would say, "Your mom and I won't always be here. Just because you are brother and sister doesn't mean when you're adults you'll be in one another lives. So if you treated one another badly in childhood, you won't want to share your lives with one another when you become adults."

He wanted us to be kind to one another, to support and love one another so we'd still be a family when he and my mom were gone.

3

Lessons in Love

FRIENDSHIPS BECAME IMPORTANT TO me early in life. My brothers would play with me, even when bank, babies, and Barbies weren't fun for them anymore. Growing up, my mom never slept over at her friends' houses; however, my dad's friends would crash at his house often. Before I was ever allowed to go to a friend's house to play, or before they were allowed to come over to spend the night, my parents would meet their parents, visit their home, talk to their parents, and exchange home telephone numbers. My parents were diligent and protective.

Violation

My parents never knew I was molested when I was four years old until I was in my late twenties. Around age seven I made a new friend. My friend came to our home to spend the night. Regrettably, I molested my friend when I introduced her to the game House my classmates taught me when I was four. She told her mother. Rightfully, her mother was furious and confronted my parents.

Looking up, I witnessed the interaction between our parents. Feelings of fear, sadness, shame, and embarrassment flooded me. The foyer at church had high ceilings, and it was early enough in the afternoon so the lights inside the building weren't on. Instead, light came in through the skylights. In the light of the afternoon sun, my parents looked down at all their children in sadness and confusion. It was a dark moment.

We went home and the whole family sat in the living room. It was time to have a family meeting.

"It's inappropriate to touch other people's bodies," Mom explained.

"I don't know who did this but it's wrong," Dad added.

I felt horrible, so I spoke up. "I'm sorry!" I cried. "I'm the one who hurt our friend. I won't ever do it again."

My mom's eyes watered. My dad looked down as his shoulders slouched, then my mom began to cry. We all went to our rooms, and we never talked about it again.

My parents never used the word *molestation*. They never asked me where I learned the behavior. They never asked if something happened to me, or why I'd done it. There were no questions asking if I'd seen anything that was inappropriate.

We didn't talk, so I never told an adult about the time an older boy kissed me at my parents' friend's house shortly before this. All the children who were older than me didn't blink an eye. Thinking it was okay, I didn't know I had been violated until I caused someone else hurt by violating them. I never acknowledged my own molestation because it was still a secret.

Over twenty years later, my parents shared the sexual trauma they experienced in their childhoods. Not only had they never shared this part of their past with one another; they never shared it with a counselor, their family, a pastor, or even a friend. Bearing the pain of their secrets alone caused them to walk in life bound in fear and shame, which lead to low self-esteem and feelings of inadequacy. Unlike this current generation, neither my parents nor their parent's were a part of an open generation. Instead, their mantra was what happens in this house stays in this house.

The secrets of their traumas caused their souls to be sick. They buried their traumas without healing from them. My parents became triggered by my act of abuse because their abuses were still haunting them. Yet back into silence they went. As long as they remained speechless in their own lives, they were unable to be a voice in my life.

At seven years old, the first message I perceived after molesting my friend was I caused hurt to her and to our families. My reasoning said I was bad person because I hurt her. My solution was to become perfect. If I was perfect, then maybe I would be a good person who wouldn't hurt anyone ever again.

To add to this already broken self-image was another conflicting message of pleasure. At such a young age, I experienced the world through my five senses. I was tormented knowing things that felt good were wrong. I concluded that not only was I bad, but I liked bad things.

Confusion set in. *Why does something bad feel good? I dare not tell someone, or they will know I am completely bad. I don't want to be bad. I want to be good.*

Without knowing it, I began attempting to give back the love I had taken from our friends through perfectionism.

Family Struggles

As the struggle within myself began, various situations troubled my family. When we first moved into our apartment, there was such a bad roach infestation that my mom would pack up our entire house multiple times so the exterminators could "bomb" our unit. She swept piles of roaches off the floor. Sometimes we'd hear whispers of people who were at our home talk about seeing roaches. For me, there was shame; it felt like people assumed we didn't maintain our home, which was far from the truth.

We lived in the suburbs; however, we weren't wealthy. A sense we didn't have enough money followed me as young as elementary school. We were on various sorts of government assistance and subsidized housing. One evening, upon returning home, I ran into my room and flipped the switch on. The light didn't turn on, so I assumed the bulb had burned out. It hadn't. Our electricity had been turned off.

In that moment, my brothers and I learned that electricity has to be *paid* for. We got in the car and went to the local outdoor and camping goods store, Army Navy Surplus. We bought a cooler and ice to keep our food cold. We bought charcoal, candles, and kerosene lanterns. My parents told us we would have to be very careful with the kerosene and the fire so we didn't burn our apartment down. My brothers and I realized how many things used electricity after ours was turned off. No turning on the stove or putting items in the refrigerator. No listening to tapes or turning on the radio.

Our apartment building had a laundry room; there were no units with private washers and dryers. Whenever we went to the store, my mom would get a roll of quarters so we could wash our clothes. My brothers and I looked forward to putting the quarters in the slots and pushing them into the machine. I recall the washer made a loud sloshing sound as it agitated the clothes. Sometimes we washed our clothes in the bathtub or sink when we couldn't afford to pay for the washers.

Getting our family from place to place became another challenge. Public transportation was an adventure, although a problematic one. We'd usually go to church, the doctor's office, and to the grocery store as a family on the bus. Our family began our journey well before we needed to be at our appointments; otherwise we'd be late or miss the appointment altogether. If a bus didn't show up or the connection to the next bus didn't happen seamlessly, the day's agenda was ruined.

I recall standing at the bus stop in all kinds of weather: the cold snow or the hot sun. Running to the bus or missing a bus that came early was irritating. My mom walked slower, so some of us walked with her. My dad had a larger gait, so if we felt energetic, we'd walk with him. Climbing the big grated metal stairs with a stroller was especially complex. We'd always be in a hurry so we wouldn't miss the bus, especially on Sundays. We caught three buses to get to church.

We rode the bus until we met our lifelong friends, the Martins, who were gracious enough to give us a ride to and from church for years. At times, we were three to a lap in Mrs. Martins blue Thunderbird. Fred Hammond was bumping and blaring through the speakers. I especially loved Mrs. Martin's three daughters. We became lifelong friends, singing, dancing, and attending concerts and revivals together.

When elementary school began, I always walked to school with Mom. In fourth grade, my friend Melissa's mom, Patti, would drive us all to and from school every day. As we got older, Jonathan and Andrew would sometimes walk with me. A few times, various families in our church gave my parents used cars so our large family could get around. The vehicles were a blessing; however, they were older vehicles and would eventually break down. Nonetheless, in our need, love from friends showed up as generosity.

The natural propensity of a child is to try and understand the world around them. I was no different. One thing about being in need is that children eventually become very aware of their household's inability and lack from a very young age. For me, this knowledge caused me to take on burdens I shouldn't have.

Most my classmates' parents owned homes and reliable vehicles. New school clothes at the beginning of the year was a guarantee for them.

My parents work too. Why are we struggling? I don't hear my classmates talking about not having electricity, water, or enough food to eat. And they certainly don't talk about roaches! Wondering why our family was different from other families troubled my mind. At the same time, my family being together in the struggle anchored me in knowing love perseveres in difficulty.

In Sickness and in Health

In elementary school, I learned a significant lesson about love from my dad. When my mom was clinically diagnosed with depression for the second time shortly after elementary school began, his love saved our family.

Being older, I was able to see the signs of her depression more clearly. First, I identified the strange look in my mom's eyes. It was as if she was there physically, but her eyes told me she was far away from us. She would cry and didn't sleep for days.

One night while my dad was working, my mom got in my bed. She was curled up, afraid and weeping. I patted her arm and gave her a hug like she'd done for me when I cried. Feeling the roles reversed and not having the confidence to take care of my mom, my default was modeling.

"It's going to be okay, Mom," I assured her.

One morning, we woke up and began getting ready for school. I was washing up in my parents' bathroom when my mom made a tearful confession.

"I swallowed a lot of pills. I didn't want to wake up. I never should have done that, Stephanie. I'm so sorry."

I looked at her and patted her hand and tried to quickly finish getting ready for school so she would have a good day.

"I forgive you," I replied.

My parents taught us to tell one another we forgave them after they apologized. I never told my dad. He was working nights, and we were there with my mom alone. I felt helpless. We all did.

My dad began to see my mom was unwell. My parents never lied to us.

"Your mom is going to a mental hospital," Dad finally said.

He attempted to keep my brothers and me together, making sure there was food in the house, that we had clean clothes, and that we got to school on time. He took all the sick time he'd accrued at work to be with us. My dad bore the weight of my mom's illness alongside her while taking care of us and working full time.

Mom was gone for what seemed to be quite a while. Years later, she shared with me that her second bout of depression was triggered by unmet expectations, unforgiveness toward my dad, and a lack of communication and financial resources. She was hurt, and it turned into anger.

Mom explained, "Our pastors came over to the house and said, 'Risa, you need to forgive. Your unforgiving heart is causing torment in your life.' I knew they were right. After this conversation and reading the book by TD Jakes called *Woman Thou Art Loosed*, I prayed and sought to forgive, then I began to get better."

This was one of the most defining moments in my life. My dad chose to stay and endure in spite of reports from the hospital, as well as the physical, mental, and emotional deterioration of my mom, his bride. It all happened right before our eyes. In such uncertain times, my dad became my rock.

Through this trial, my dad exemplified 1 Corinthians 13:7–8 where Paul described love as bearing all things, believing all things, hoping all things, and enduring all things. "Love never fails."

A New Church

When my mom came back from the hospital, we began attending a new church. Initially, I felt out of place because we didn't know anyone. The first time we visited, my family and our pastor's family went to dinner together. My dad told our new pastor how I wanted to feed homeless people.

Our new pastor and his wife listened intently, and as a church we began feeding breakfast to 120-plus people on Sunday mornings in downtown Denver where he pastored his church. We got to know our new church family quickly because we worked together cooking, cleaning, and serving others.

At our new church my mom began coaching a Bible quiz team. Teams of children memorized scriptures and would be quizzed on what they'd learned by competing against other church teams in our region. My mom became my coach, and we began to bond. We spent a lot of time memorizing scriptures through songs we made up and practicing. I got pretty good winning competitions within my team and in the state. My mom loved the Bible. She would hold it close to her heart and close her eyes as we recited the scriptures. Peace finally began to surround our family.

My brothers and I grew up in church. We attended church twice on Sundays and faithfully attended midweek services on Wednesday evenings. My family joined prayer meetings on Tuesdays. We met our lifelong friends there, the Ulibarris. Tuesday night prayer meetings were held in their living room.

They were a beautiful family—hospitable, hilarious, godly, and real. They honored God in a way that set them apart from most people.

I connected with the older Ulibarri girls. We visited one another's homes, attended birthday parties, made up songs, and put homemade face masks on. Our childhood was filled with going to Goodwill (also known as the *Segunda*), catching frogs and crawdads from the creek near my house, and being told not to go near the sinking, stinking mud at the beginning of the pond behind our house. Some of us were better listeners than others! Waking up at six in the morning with Natalie to clean her pets' cages was quite an experience! Our families spent so much time together, they became our family too.

One place my family could guarantee being together was at church. My dad taught the adults on Sunday mornings, and my mom taught Sunday school. They both are very empathetic and caring toward others and often prayed with people. We heard powerful messages all the time. My greatest desire was to experience abundance and peace, the kind we heard about in sermons. It was more than a hope; I needed it to become a reality.

We often heard amazing testimonies of people being betrayed and choosing to forgive those who hurt them. We even heard of people being delivered from alcoholism and drugs and beginning a new life in Jesus. It was hard to relate to their testimonies because we grew up rolling under pews or sleeping on top of them. Even so, the stories were still beautiful. In this season of our lives, love meant caring for and connecting to others.

Beginning Adolescence

One of my favorite memories was attending youth camp in the summer. We always had an incredible time. All the messages were geared toward young people. We played games, sprinted and tumbled through obstacle courses, listened to music, sang, laughed, and heard testimonies from our counselors into the wee hours of the morning. They were wonderful women. We had bonfires, bought snacks from the canteen, participated in Bible quiz tournaments, and went to Bible study every morning.

While listening to the sermons and Bible studies, I wished to hear about someone like me. But never was one message given about sexual trauma, or ways to overcome the mistakes of premature sexual experiences. I longed for someone's story I could relate to. There wasn't a place to talk about my abuse, so I didn't. This burden was one I ended up carrying alone; it got heavier as the years passed.

The transition from childhood to adolescence was a difficult one. I was a year older than all my classmates because my birthday was in October. More nuances came with my transition and became particularly hard because I physically developed faster than my classmates.

When my chest first started developing, my mom emphatically announced to me as I was getting ready for school, "Girl, you need a bra!"

Once again, she picked up a book to explain my development to me instead of her personal experience. The book talked about women's bodies and menstrual cycles and what a baby looked like when it was in the womb. My mom wasn't the only one who noticed my changing body. I began hearing rumors at school.

Olivia, one of my best friends, said, "Ellie told us at recess that she thinks you stuff your bra."

I looked at her, confused and unaware of what *stuffing* was. "What does stuffing your bra mean?" I asked.

"Stuffing your bra is when you fill it with tissue," Olivia explained.

I looked at her, appalled. The thought never crossed my mind. We walked into our classroom and sat at our desks. A thought flashed across my mind: *What if I lift up my shirt and show little Ellie and the other gossiping girls the truth? No, I'll just be in more trouble.* Once the hurt and anger left, I sat at my desk and cried. *I thought they were my friends.*

Friendship and jealousy cannot reside in the same heart. Feelings of self-conscious about my body increased once my classmates' whispers were brought into the light. Boys shared thoughts about my changing body, too, further solidifying my insecurity. At church I was becoming friends with a new girl who had older brothers. One of her brothers was closer to our age and he was attractive.

I spent the night at her house, and the next morning we were getting ready in the bathroom when she exclaimed, "Dang, girl! You got a big chest!"

I was caught off guard by her comment.

"My brother even said that he thinks you have a nice chest. He doesn't think your pretty though," she added.

She kept on chatting. I swallowed hard and forced myself to stop listening. Subconsciously, I wrote her statement down on a notecard and safely stored it away in the Rolodex of my mind: *You have a nice chest, but you're not pretty.*

Thankfully, Aunt Jean and Aunt Kathy were amazing. Their kindness and concern prevented my self–esteem from being eliminated. Aunt Kathy helped create one of the only positive memories I have about becoming a young woman.

She took my cousins, Jinnelle and Celeste, and me shopping. We wandered through the isles until we got to the women's intimates' section of the store. Aunt Kathy kindly offered to purchase me bra and underwear sets.

My cousins told me which patterns were cute. Aunt Kathy smiled in approval. This was the first and last time I celebrated my changing body. The experience felt like a rite of passage of sorts. All my aunts complimented me on my clothes, or my height, or gave suggestions with a product whether it was lotion, or a nail polish, thanks Aunt Jean.

Sadness and anger were often emotions I carried because of my new, changing body based on how my peers perceived it. Puberty was tougher than any book described. Not talking about the rumors or other negative experiences seemed to be the right decision because I was embarrassed. Concealment only last so long before the effects showed up in my lack of love for my temple.

PART 2

SEEKING LOVE

4

The Impact of Love

LOVE CONTINUED TO GROW in our family, even when I was experiencing a personally confusing time growing up. When my mom was pregnant with my third brother, Matthew, my greatest desire was for my parents to have a girl. While my mom was in the hospital, we stayed at my Aunt Jean and Uncle Omar's house. Aunt Jean and I have a great connection. Spending the night at their house and visiting with them and my three older boy cousins was a true joy. My auntie gave me my first purse. I chose a big, red one. I loved it! Uncle Omar gave me a dollar every time he saw me wearing it. Their sons were equally as engaging.

Cousin Micha always laughed, talked, and played with my brothers and me all day long it seemed. At times, I'd watch shows with my cousin Armon. He would always suggest I didn't watch talk shows. Our cousin Damon was lively; he talked fast and laughed often.

On solo rides with Aunt Jean, she'd ask me how school was, ask about my friends, ask about family stuff, and ask about any activities I was involved in. Her intentionality was impeccable. Over the next few days, we cooked a lot. Our mouths tingled with the tartness of the rhubarb we cut from her garden. She often took my brothers, cousins, and me to the movies, out to eat, or shopping. I always felt seen and safe at my Uncle Omar and Aunt Jean's house.

Growing Love

While waiting for the baby to be born, Jonathan, Andrew, and I went to the library with my aunt and uncle one day and saw a fascinating bug exhibit. When we arrived home and walked in their house, there was a message flashing on the answering machine.

I put the earpiece next to my ear. "We had a boy! His name is Matthew Anthony!" my dad said. I dropped my head and gave the phone back to my aunt.

Desire for a sister was strong. I wanted a built-in best friend like my two younger brothers found in one another. Someone I could play Barbies with. Someone to do each other's hair. Over time, I got over it. Matthew became our happy, hilarious brother.

My cousins and brothers taught him phrases like, "Talk to the hand, 'cause the face ain't listenin'," and "Raise the roof!"

Five years later on a cold day in February, my youngest brother was born. Nine months prior, my parents told us they were expecting another baby boy. I was in shock. By this time, I was twelve. My brothers and I sat in Grandma Murray's bedroom and watched TV after school while we waited for our newest brother to be born. Hours passed, and before I knew it, we'd missed our midweek church service.

Our brother must have been born since we missed church, I thought.

My parents fifth and final child, Josiah David, was born February 10. He was a cute baby with light-brown eyes, curly hair, and deep dimples. He was happy, and we all doted over him in our own way. Our three-bedroom apartment was bursting at the seams, so my parents decided it was time for us to move again.

I was now in middle school. On our morning walks to school, we were greeted with the most beautiful sunrises and an unobstructed view of the Rocky Mountains. The mountains were so clear and appeared in close enough proximity one could walk to them in just a day.

At my new school, I stayed to myself at first. My backpack was especially heavy with the binder, planner, and books. Navigating through the halls and going from classroom to classroom was new. I liked most of my teachers and joined band for the first time. I chose the flute because I was inspired by my friend Annette from church. She was a gifted musician and songwriter. With no new friends yet, I would hurry home after school and practice my flute nonstop to pass the time and dispel the feelings of loneliness.

One day in gym in early fall I made my first friend.

The gym teacher said, "You're all going to run a mile. You need to get it done in under fifteen minutes . . . Go!"

I was perplexed. *A whole mile!*

I began walking when I heard, "Hey, let's run!"

I'd really planned on walking at first; however, my classmate seemed friendly enough, and walking would take longer to finish the mile, so I obliged.

My classmate's name was Natelie. I soon found out she was a caring and straightforward person. Although she embodied a motherly disposition, she didn't coddle people. Instead, she was honest and encouraging. She reminded me of my god sister, Natalie, in so many ways; it was astounding. The first time Natelie told me about myself, what she said stung, yet I needed to hear it.

Although I didn't have biological sisters, I referred to the Martin sisters from church as my sisters because I wanted sisters, and I basically grew up with these girls. In our church, we greeted adults as sister and brother so-in-so. Over the years, I called these friends of mine sisters so often that people believed I had female siblings.

Natelie and I were getting ready to walk into the lunchroom as I was telling a story about my "sisters," when she stopped me from talking midsentence. She whipped her head around with a slight frown said, "Hey, you really shouldn't call your friends your sisters. You don't have any sisters, and when you say sisters it gives people the impression you do and you come off as a liar."

I was a taken back, so I looked down and shuffled my feet. She was right. Right then I stopped calling my friends my sisters. Natelie taught me a loving friendship can only exist and grow in the truth, and by God's goodness we are still best friends today.

Best Friends

Natelie exuded confidence. She was an excellent student and artist. Her sarcasm made me laugh hard every day. She spoke matter-of-factly about everything. We started having slumber parties, watching TV, listening to music, talking about boys at school, and eating snacks out of her pantry. Her pantry was the best, and once I went to Costco with her family, I understood why.

She only lived a few blocks from my house, so sometimes we would walk to school together. Walking together only lasted a little while though. Natelie is what I call a romantic walker. I, on the other hand, walk quickly like my dad, especially in the hot summer sun or on a cold winter afternoon.

It was fine; neither Natelie nor I got easily offended about things. We weren't possessive over one another's choices or friends. We gave one another license to be ourselves and do what we wanted. There weren't any obligations; we were just there for one another. We were friends, plain and simple. Soon, Natelie became my best friend.

Only because God is fantastically good is why I can even describe what happened for the second time in sixth grade. I met another friend named Katie. She and I met in social studies. Our first assignment was to partner up and create an imaginary country. Even then, group projects weren't my favorite, especially because I didn't know the work ethic of my classmates yet. Nonetheless, I was partnered up with Katie. We completed the project effortlessly and got along great.

Katie and I shared a similar temperament, yet she was carefree. I laughed a lot with Katie, mostly at nothing and at the same time everything. Nothing was too intense or serious when we were together because she loved to have fun. Snow days, bikes, and dogs were her favorite things. We went to the movies and to the mall together too.

One day when I was at her house, I think we were supposed to be working on a project together; however, we ended up in a glitter fight! My whole family had tiny pieces of glitter in their hair, on their skin, and on their clothes for months after I got home. Over the years, we were in different friend groups and had different interests; however, we established a genuine friendship and made an effort to be in each other's lives from then until now.

My relationships with Natelie and Katie are still filled with love. Thankfully, envy, jealousy, and ill will never entered into the fabric of these relationships that have lasted over twenty years.

Saturday School

Around this time, my dad reunited with his old neighbor friend, Mrs. Jackson. My dad met her and her incredible family the first year of he and my mom's marriage. Mrs. Jackson became one of the most spiritual and influential teachers in my life. She was a phenomenal woman. Not only was she friendly, with A-plus integrity, she spoke plainly and honestly. Not many people can make others feel like they are important every time they are in their presence; yet she did because of how observant, attentive, and caring she was.

Whenever I asked my parents a question, they never lied to me. yet, Mrs. Jackson took it a step further; she was transparent. I could ask her questions; and she was proactive about sharing her full story. Her love prepared and warned me of the dangers ahead. Mrs. Jackson taught me that the highest form of honesty is transparency and vulnerability.

She was transparent about her previous struggles and vulnerable about her current ones. She was one of the freest people I knew because she was bold. One of my favorite illustrations she used was the picture of an eye with tears streaming down.

"If you don't have a criteria, you are going to cry!" she said.

In the years to come I would find out what she meant.

My brothers, cousin and I attended her FUTURE (For You to Understand Real Economics) class and her Black history courses on Saturdays with about a dozen other children. She would teach us anywhere from two to three hours an afternoon. She was excited and prepared every week.

In her FUTURE class, we learned about credit, banking, business ownership, check writing as well as the basics of savings and checking accounts. In her Black history class, we learned about the men and women who went before us. We learned we were a part of a powerful, fearless, and intelligent race of people. Her smile and presence impacted everyone she met. And still, I'll never forget the time her lack of a smile impacted me the most.

One morning, she woke up with symptoms of Bell's palsy. She couldn't smile. Bell's palsy is described as a sudden, temporary weakness in a person's facial muscles. This makes half the face appear to droop. A person's smile is one-sided, and the eye on that side resists closing. Mrs. Jackson could have cancelled class. Instead, she taught us all one of the greatest lessons about love and life I'd ever hear.

Immediately, when I walked into the classroom, I knew something was different. The excitement that was usually in the room wasn't there. Nonetheless, I could still feel the passion Mrs. Jackson possessed.

There's no way my classmates and I could ever know what was going to happen next. We sensed in our spirits this class was going to be different. Mrs. Jackson came to class in a long gown, her hair in a night turban, and no makeup. The class came in and sat down quietly. She didn't greet us with her usual greetings. We looked attentively toward her and the whiteboard at the front of her basement classroom.

She began to talk the best she could. "Today I woke up and my face was sagging. I was diagnosed with Bell's palsy. Have any of you ever heard of Bell's palsy?

We all shook our heads side to side. I sat up straighter in my chair and my heart began to beat faster.

In true teacher fashion, Mrs. Jackson explained to us what the disease was. "I'm not aware of when or if the muscles in my face and jaw will regain strength."

Next, she showed us how difficult it was for her to drink water. She would take a drink, and the water would simultaneously seep out of her drooping jaw and cheek. She held a towel up to her face as she drank.

She described and showed us various symptoms. With a quivering voice she said, "What I'm most concerned about is not being able to smile again. Today, I'm going to tell you about my husband, Mr. Jackson. It's important to love others and to be loved."

Throughout the rest of class, she spoke of her husband. We listened as she described how he loved her unconditionally, especially in her sickness. Without her usual smile, makeup, fancy clothes, or a sleek hairstyle, he still loved her.

"It's always been and will always be about who you are inside, not possessions or your looks." Mrs. Jackson taught all of us that love keeps promises.

I left Mrs. Jackson's classroom forever changed and wondering, *Was the love I possessed never-failing? Would it withstand pressure, unexpected sickness, financial troubles, and life-changing challenges? Is it possible to love and be loved unconditionally, like I'd witnessed from my parents and heard about through Mrs. Jackson's testimony of her marriage this Saturday afternoon?* I held these questions close to my heart.

Drill Team

Within the year, we were visiting Grandma Murray's house when we heard drums outside. The drums were loud, and the sound ricocheted off the brick wall ball arena and the surrounding houses in the cul-de-sac. My parents and I went across the street to the Red Shield Community Center in Denver. My parents found out Mrs. Jackson's daughter, Mrs. Page, was beginning the second generation of the Colorado Starlites drill team. We went over to see them.

I will never forget the first time I walked into the Starlites' practice room. The room was filled to the brim with energy. Every person stood in place. There were girls younger and older than me lined up in perfect rows, four lines across and eight rows back, looking straight ahead.

Every girl followed Mrs. Page's command. "Just breathe, blink, and look forward."

They were so in unison, they looked like one person. Their body language spoke to me. It said power, togetherness, unity, and order.

Mrs. Page's voice commanded the room: "Drill team, attention!"

She pronounced every syllable in every word perfectly. The sound made the hairs on the back of my neck stand up, and it intensified when I saw thirty-plus girls from ages four to nineteen in unison stomp their right foot. It was one precise motion and sound. No one's foot hit the ground after everyone else's landed. It was perfect. Mrs. Page called out other steps, and everyone performed them together. It was pristine.

I was in awe of all of them. I wanted to join, yet I didn't know if I could do what I'd seen them do. "Do you want to be a part of the team?" a coach asked me.

I nodded wide-eyed, and said, "Yes, ma'am."

There was a system where the new girls practiced upstairs. One of the coaches taught us "the basics." Every Wednesday, the newest girls would go down to the team's main practice room to be assessed on what we'd learned. Our coach would call the steps, and we would do them to the best of our ability. At first, we'd be so nervous we would mess up, regardless of how well we did. At the end, our teammates would clap for us. I would leave practice on Wednesday and practice all week long. I loved drill team. I strived to be worthy of the room downstairs; I wanted to be one with them. Eventually, my practice paid off.

Mrs. Page would have different people who knew the steps or created them do one-on-one coaching with those who were still struggling. This is how I met Cecile. Her smile was bright, and she laughed easily, she knew everyone's name. Cecile was magnetic; people were drawn to her, both good and bad. Cecile was becoming a dancer, and stepping came easy to her. As Cecile helped teach me and our other teammates the steps, she was very gracious and encouraging. Cecile became a fun, consistent friend in my life, and still is today.

Usually, when the team would learn a new step in practice, I wouldn't get it the entire time we were in the practice. Then my family would get in the car to go to church, and I would practice it in my mind. As I counted, I would move my toes up and down in my shoes. As soon as we pulled up to church, I would jump out of the car to see if I knew the step. Nine times out of ten I did and would continue to practice the rest of the week.

The second generation Starlites wore purple and white to represent royalty and purity. We stood tall, proud, and respectful. We won all sorts of awards and competed in competitions all over Colorado. Mrs. Page's team consisted of a drill team, drummers, pom poms, flags, and a stomp team. You should have seen the amount of people in awe when ninety children and twenty coaches and parents came into restaurants silently and sat down to eat dinner when we went away on trips.

Mrs. Page was a phenomenal leader. She led with her family, including her daughter, Mrs. T, and sister, Mrs. Terri, and many friends, including Mrs. Jones and Mrs. Lynn. Mrs. Page was greatly supported by her husband, Mr. Page, and her father, Mr. Jackson.

Upon entering the room, Mrs. Page reminded us, "You can't come into this room until you're willing to give 110 percent!" She taught us about discipline, unity, and character. Her walk was one of excellence.

Her standards were high and her character was impeccable. In addition to Mrs. Page, the coaches and team parents, like Ms. Perrin, gave their all. How she knew us was commendable. She not only knew our names, she knew our temperaments, strengths, and weaknesses. Although she often corrected us, her celebration of us was astounding. We were proud to be Starlites.

During one of our trips to California, we were supposed to be in a televised parade. Unfortunately, upon returning to the hotel, it was explained to us the organization we were supposed to be marching with didn't want us marching with them. To say we were hurt would be an understatement.

Tears flowed down my teammates' faces. Personally, I was in shock. The leaders and staff spoke. At the end, they asked if any of us wanted to share. I raised my hand. Usually I'm a slow processor, yet in the moment words filled me.

"I have been a part of the Starlites for the past six years," I began. "The Starlites always lead parades. In every competition we entered, we were usually in the top three places. We have dozens of trophies and awards. And still over all these years, we have never cried together. We have only trained, laughed, performed, and celebrated together. Today we cried together. So today, I believe we became a team."

Even then, my heart knew only through adversity could one say the bond of love shared was of value. Mrs. Page and all the love from the coaches, parents, and staff showed up as a covering in their discipline, patience in their teaching, a shout in their celebration, and a hope we wouldn't only shine with the Starlites; we would shine in our lives.

5

Is This Love?

KIDS WERE ALWAYS HOLDING hands and kissing in the hallways in middle school. It was strange at first. Yet after every passing year, PDA became normal. All the popular boys had girlfriends. Rumors made their way around at recess. People whispered about what certain couples did when their parents weren't around.

Kids started to steal liquor from their parents' liquor cabinets. Some lost their virginity, and some pitched their money in with their older siblings to get access to a variety of drugs and alcohol. As time went on, I identified less and less with my peers.

Naivety

Repeatedly, various people said they observed my maturity. Wanting to be an adult, I heard this as a compliment. Adulthood would afford me the freedom to determine the destiny of my life in every area, including relationships and finances. I craved this affirmation. Even as a young person, people found it easy to confide in me. Countless times, people would just sit and talk to me. As I listened intently, their words would tumble out at first, then they would flow like a river.

In almost every conversation, people would realize they'd been talking for hours and abruptly stop talking and ask, "How old are you?"

I would tell them my age, and their brows would furrow in confusion.

"You're so mature for your age," they would say, then continue their conversation.

A variety of compliments followed. Being a more reserved child and the oldest of my peers at school, I often heard, "You carry yourself well," or "You're really smart" or "You have a good head on your shoulders."

Adults trusted me and saw me as a good kid overall. Not flawless, but good. How others perceived me was immensely important to me. My self-esteem and pride hung on others' opinions of me. I basked in the approval of others because I felt so low. In the inevitable quietness, my feelings of goodness were tempered in the fear of people finding out about me being molested and molesting other children when I was younger.

Feverishly, I grabbed ahold of anything good people said about me because there were not enough good things I meditated on within myself. I constantly worked hard on creating a sea of my own goodness so the boulder-like heaviness I felt from my sins could one day be tossed into the sea of forgetfulness (Micah 7:19). If only I could forget though.

Coming from a large family, having a father and all male siblings caused me to believe I had an advantage over other girls my age when it came to boys and men. Now don't get me wrong; I did have a different perspective and understanding of maleness than my peers who were fatherless and didn't have brothers. Yet an overestimated perception of my understanding of maleness hurt me.

Unwisely, I believed that as people grow older they stay as honest as young children. In ignorance, I began accepting advances of adolescent boys who showed interest and affection toward me. This was my state of mind in seventh grade when I dated my first boyfriend.

Adolescent Relationships

My family and I went to visit some of my parents' friends one evening. Soon after we arrived, all the children went into a room to watch a movie. We sprawled out all over the room, and I ended up sitting close to a boy I'd known for many years named DJ. Never paying much attention to DJ before, he looked different now, probably because he was older.

As the night progressed, DJ kept paying me attention, then he kissed me. Surprised, I shrunk back at first. The kiss was nice, though, so I kissed him back. His kiss gave me validation. *Maybe what my friend's brother said about me isn't true? Maybe I am pretty. Maybe I've changed in the last year.*

The movie ended, and we all went outside to walk along a trail behind their house. DJ and I kissed a few more times. Prior to this day, I had fantasized about having a boyfriend and kissing him. The furthest my fantasy got was kissing. I never considered what would happen after exchanging kisses. I quickly found out my body didn't have boundaries. His hands travelled below my waist. His touches felt good, and I touched him too.

Later on he asked, "Do you want to be my girlfriend?"

"Yes," I replied without thinking.

After we left DJ's house, I went home and considered what happened, and regret set in. A day passed, and my parents could clearly see something was wrong. Guilt caused me not to want to talk about it, along with my fear and embarrassment.

"Can I go talk to Logan?" I asked my parents one evening. They were puzzled, but they nodded their agreement.

Logan was a classmate of mine who lived up the street from us. She met me in front of my house and when I saw her I burst into tears after telling her what happened, and she patted me on the back. What brought me the most angst was the thought of ending up in the pastor's office with my parents if they found out. I felt afraid.

Little did I know my parents were watching this interaction with my friend through the front window of our house. They were furious. Once I got home, they confronted me.

"Stephanie, don't confide in your friend about what's going on with you when your mom and I asked you what was wrong and you chose not to share it with us," Dad said. "That's unfair and very hurtful!"

I confessed my actions to them.

My parents were appalled. Then began the questions.

"What were you thinking?" Dad asked. "Why would you be conducting yourself like that when you were supposed to be hanging out with a group of friends?"

I knew I'd disappointed them and broke their trust. Answers remained buried inside and were never uttered, so through the tears all I mustered was, "I'm sorry."

Days later, a friend of mine called and asked, "Are you still with DJ?"

Cautiously, I replied, "Yes."

Reluctantly, she spoke up, "Oh, well today he asked me to be his girlfriend."

Honestly, relief washed over me. I wasn't hurt, so I just called and told him, "I don't want to be with you anymore." As quickly as it started, it ended.

One would think my first dating experience would deter me from adolescent relationships for a while, but it didn't.

In adolescence, the seed of perversion planted in my child-hood through the traumas I experienced grew stronger and taller. Putting myself in compromising situations felt good in the moment; afterward, though, it always filled me with a lot of shame. With my innocence gone, it was almost as if attracting young people who were also broken became the norm. A boyfriend to me was validation of my attractiveness, both physically and mentally.

Sam

I met Sam in eighth grade. He was tall and charismatic and made friends easily. Sam was from the East Coast, and I loved his accent. He was a year younger than me, and we went to school together. One day Sam asked me for my number, and we talked on the phone; however, we saw one another more often.

When we walked in the hall together, his long arm dangled down the side of my shoulder and torso. We didn't kiss in the hallways at school. I wasn't that bold. I knew those kids were wild. And besides, what if my parents or Grandma LaVonne popped up? They'd never popped up before, but they could! The passionate kisses we shared were always in private when we'd go places together, not in our homes.

We went to a school dance together with my cousin Malia, who was new to the school. He called Malia his cousin too, just for fun. We weren't alone often, which was good. Sam was growing out his hair, so he came over to my house one day, and my cousin braided his hair. We did all sorts of things together: went to the mall, to plays at church, to the park, and to the store with our parents. We also had fun together in groups.

Most boys where we lived showed more interest in my friends and bypassed me, further reinforcing my fear of being unattractive. There weren't many Black girls or boys where we lived and attended school. So even after Sam began irritating me, I made the decision to stay with him out of "boyfriend scarcity" and low self-esteem.

Irritation began with him pressuring me to be more physical, but I wasn't comfortable going further. He started treating me differently, acting rude and uninterested. Then he tried to approach my friend, so we broke up. My assessment was that because he was younger than me, he was immature.

From that point on, I never dated anyone younger than me. I attributed my irritation of him more to his age, not his persistent pushing of my boundaries. My solution was to date boys who were older than me. Asking my parents' permission to date was never a conversation because I knew they would disapprove, so everything I did was in secret.

Ethan

Ethan was seventeen and I was fourteen when our relationship began. Ethan's beautiful light-brown eyes and handsome features caught my attention. Showing my friends his picture was met with nods of approval, followed by, "He's cute." His interest in me for a short season quieted my thoughts that he was out of my league.

Leaning in for a kiss he'd say, "I love your lips and your smile."

Hearing approval about my appearance soothed the fears of the girl who's heard, "She's not pretty. She has a nice chest though." Never had I acknowledged what I believed was beautiful about me before hearing someone else's assessment of me.

When we had been too passionate and flirtatious with one another, Ethan said, "Don't start something you can't finish."

Although compromising the Christian values my parents were instilling in me, it was still important to me to keep my virginity at the time, and he respected my decision.

Besides attraction, Ethan and I weren't aligned in any way.

A couple of times he came to my church. We lived far away from each other, and neither of us drove so, we hung out when and where we could. To further our alienation, Ethan dropped out of high school. Even though he was being encouraged to go to school and get his GED, he wasn't following through. Not being a part of his life a long time, what surprised me were the feelings of disappointment I possessed when he didn't pursue finishing his education. Over time, I found out why he lacked hope, ambition, and dreams.

Ethan was an alcoholic. Never having smoked or drank, the signs were foreign to me. Also, I didn't live with parents who ever drank alcohol. His body had become swollen, and other times his eyes were bloodshot, indicating his addict life-style. There were multiple times we'd be on the phone and he'd be so drunk, he'd throw up.

In his drunken clarity, he would say, "I need to stop drinking."

Distraught and ill-equipped to help him, one Sunday afternoon I begged him, "Please, don't drink today!"

"It's Sunday night, the game is on. I'm going to enjoy myself. You understand, right?" he replied.

Understanding wasn't in me. His lack of drive and desire to do anything good with his life was causing him to spiral downward fast. A few weeks passed, and my cousin Malia told me she saw Ethan with another girl. I cried uncontrollably. I felt pain in my chest as if my heart was imploding on itself. All the R&B songs speaking of heartbreak made sense; caring for someone with the inability to help themselves and being hurt by them was heavy.

6

The Deconstruction
of Love

ON THE OUTSIDE, MY family appeared fairly normal and intact. What people may not have noticed was how angry we all were. Because Dad worked nights, it put a strain on all of our relationships with him and amongst ourselves, mostly because there was a lack of communication and quality time with him. Also, the financial strain we experienced as children continued into our adolescence.

Lack

Resentment and frustration began to build between my dad and us kids. Imperative conversations weren't had. Time spent together was at church and not as a family playing games or eating dinners. When my brothers and I played sports or received awards, my dad's work hours didn't allow him to be physically present to see our achievements or cheer us on from the stands. Asking for necessities like contacts, socks, shoes, or clothes would begin angry, resentful fights between my mom, my siblings, and me. She was the only one there to hear all our complaints.

Being in lack caused our family great anxiety. It was hard, it was uncertain, and it became exhausting over the years.

Our financial struggles were frustrating because my parents worked hard and didn't lack effort. Yet as a family, we kept finding ourselves without. Why? Because dreaming of business ownership without business training, a lack of fair compensation, and a lack of longevity on jobs does not lead to financial success. And still, bill collectors called.

It was like we gave up quality time with our parents without reaping adequate financial benefits in return. When there was abundance, like tax return season, we were good for only a short time. My family needed so much that my parents quickly used their refund for our necessities. Then we'd begin the struggle again for another year.

What was causing anger and turmoil was the lack of love we all felt. I know for me, I longed for a better connection with my parents and brothers. I wanted to spend time together outside of church, to have a vision and common goal, and to experience more support in the day-to-day tasks. I desired to share proud, fun moments with my family more regularly. And I wanted to experience the ease of not struggling financially.

Goodness

And still, during these difficult times we experienced the kindness of people in ways we never imagined. Growing up in the summer, my brothers played street hockey and basketball with our neighbor's son, David. They were always outside playing a sport, building a clubhouse, or a go-kart out of scrap wood, or crawling through the grass in the backyard in their army fatigues.

As told to me by my brother Jonathan: "It was summer, and David, Andrew, and I wanted to swim in the pool in our backyard, but it was low on water. David went over to the hose and turned it on. Nothing came out. Andrew and I admitted our water had been turned off. A little while later David went home. Then later in the afternoon he came back and our water was on."

My mom's speculations from all those years ago were right. Our neighbors paid for our water to be turned back on. They never told us. We would have gladly thanked them and acknowledged them. Yet their act of love was so pure, it began and ended in helping us, not in them being recognized. We kept our dignity. Our neighbor's gift to us was free. Goodness was given and received.

One December, the fire and police departments brought us gifts for Christmas. Multiple times my brother's coach, Matt, and his family paid for my brother's sport fees, bought them food after games, and purchased them a gaming console after Andrew was injured. One year, they bought our entire family coats and Christmas presents.

All these experiences developed a deep sense of compassion within me. Being grateful and genuinely happy when people exceled or received what they needed was embedded in me.

Breaking Down to Build Up

Between fourteen and fifteen, my mom was hospitalized for depression for the last time. Before we saw the signs, I felt God speak to my heart to fast for three days. This was the first fast I completed by myself. It started on Monday and ended on Wednesday. It was almost winter break, and my brothers and I were looking forward to being out of school. Wednesday night I saw the telltale signs.

My parents drove a passenger van and picked people up all over the city for church; afterward, they dropped them back at home. We were in the van on our way to a friend's house when signs of my mom's depression came flooding back. My mom was extremely emotional. She was crying a lot, and bags rested underneath her eyes. Phrases she said were partly coherent. She struggled to communicate with us and hold everything together at the same time.

It was Christmas Day, and we were continuing in my parents' family's traditions: brunch with my mom's side and dinner on my dad's side. This particular year, my mom's family was coming to our house for Christmas brunch. She was stressed. We didn't have much of a Christmas, and the household finances weren't good. Being overwhelmed with it all caused my mom to break down crying. Within moments, it was decided Grandma Lavonne would take my mom to the hospital. I began crying, and Aunt Collette hugged me tight and prayed over me and our family. Her prayer brought peace in the chaos.

We all began to help around the house more than we usually did. All of us stepped up to be there for one another and relieve our dad's stress. Waking up the next morning, it was obvious that everything from the day before was still fresh. We all got ready for church somberly without Mom.

At church my friend Candice came over to me and gushed, "What'd you get for Christmas?"

I shrugged. "To be honest, I just want my mom to get out of the hospital."

Not knowing what to say, she offered, "At least . . ."

I didn't hear anything else Candice said. Looking at her coldly, tears streamed down my face.

An older woman in our church came over and asked, "Why are you crying?"

I briefly explained what Candice said. The older woman tried to console me, but I was angry. Minutes later, after her parents scolded her, Candice tearfully came over to apologize.

Forgiving her was easy. I didn't have the energy to be upset with her. Even though we were both young, observation taught me she didn't understand what I was going through. Soon I found myself wishing I was at home while simultaneously knowing that's not what we did on Sundays. The Murrays were committed to God's house. We were there whether it rained or poured, whether we were happy and getting along or arguing and fighting as a family.

My parents' example impacted me, especially my mom, who prayed, sang, and worshipped with all her heart, even if our electricity was turned off, or the gas light in our car was bright red, or when there wasn't enough food, or if the water was off and my parents had to bring jugs of water home from work so we could flush the toilet, bathe, or cook. My mom's worship never changed. She remained exuberant, passionate, vulnerable, and honest at every church service.

Holding onto Hope

Weeks later, one afternoon my mom came with Grandma LaVonne to visit us for a few hours. There was a great chasm between us. It was as if we were meeting a stranger for the first time. The woman in the living room wasn't my mother. Medication numbed her. After Grandma LaVonne dropped my mom back off at the hospital, we all went to Grandma Murray's house for dinner.

While we were there, Grandma LaVonne asked us how we felt about seeing our mom. We all shifted our weight, leaning from one foot to the other in uncomfortable silence. No one made eye contact. We were just finishing dinner and got up to scrape our plates and clean the table.

Eventually, I broke the silence. "I don't know. I feel like Mom seemed like a zombie."

Grandma LaVonne was very straightforward and to the point. At this time in my life, I didn't know how to swallow stiff drinks of truth. "Well, your mom may be on medication the rest of her life, and your dad should talk to you about that!" she revealed.

I was furious, and tears rolled down my cheeks. We all needed Mom back, but not the shell of her.

Not daring to say it out loud, inside I shouted, *She's not going to be on medication the rest of her life! And don't criticize my dad! He's doing the best he can. Plus, he's all we've got!*

Attempting to respect my grandmother by not arguing or debating with her, tears expressed the unspoken words of my heart.

Then the juxtaposition ensued with Grandma Murray saying, "Don't cry,"

Grandma LaVonne chimed in with, "No, let her cry!"

They were both right. I needed to cry, and then it would be time to wipe my tears and do the best I could every day. In this season, love looked like exemplifying tenacious hope and moving forward despite setbacks.

Even though I didn't know it then, I was right too. Love meant holding onto the hope that my mom would get better even if others didn't see it or believe it. It also meant lifting up and appreciating my dad for doing his best.

Whenever my mom came back from the hospital, the dynamic of our home changed. Dad was working and trying his best to make sure we had what we needed at home. My brothers and I took care of one another the best we could. We all tried to keep our rhythm in school and with our extracurricular activities while helping around the house more.

As for Mom, she started talking instead of keeping her frustration and hurt inside. Our pastor's wife helped her find natural herbs to help balance her hormones so she could get off the medications. Little by little, she stopped taking the medication.

In recent conversations with my mom, she clarified some things. "I decided I was going to have to fight the thoughts and feelings that caused me to be angry, unforgiving, and isolated in our familial relationships and in my life. These thoughts and feelings led me into cycles of hurt, pain, and depression. Particularly, I had to reject every thought that told me you all were better off without me."

My mom's determination to fight to become who God created her to be is admirable. The battle with depression could only be won with God's loving word, a supportive family and community, and my mom's decision to fight.

It's been years since we've seen distance in my mother's eyes. We're fortunate to have my mom back in our lives as a whole person, and nothing can express the gratitude we have toward God and the happiness we feel seeing her interactions with our family and friends. Her wholeness created platforms where she was able to share her story with the world through keynote speaking at a gala, and through her art and teaching.

Through these experiences of long-suffering in relationships and financial woes, love showed up as support, healing, forgiveness, and celebrating one another through our adversities.

7

Without Love

FRESHMAN YEAR IN HIGH school I had a chip on my shoulder. At the beginning of the year, it felt as if everything had changed over the summer. After learning my best friend, Natelie, was going to a different high school, anxiety and fear flooded me. Perceptions that my classmates from middle school were acting like brand-new kids prevented me from seeing I was new too. We'd all changed. In many ways, we'd not changed for the better.

"Freshman year you were angry," Katie told me recently. "You pretty much just stomped around from class to class."

Embarrassed, all I could do was nod; she was right.

Freshman Year

Feelings of loneliness and anger plagued me because of all the social changes at school. Trying to be a Christian as a teenager at school and not relating to my peers left me feeling alone. Was everyone drinking, smoking, experimenting with drugs, and having sex?

Knowing my life was different from my classmates' lives mentally but not yet experientially stopped me from being invested in my school on a relational and emotional level. My heart was at home, where my family was still rebounding after my mom's last bout with depression. Furthermore, my cousin Malia moved in with us during the current school year because she was struggling in school and kept running away from home, and we'd just found out she was pregnant.

As a family, we all had a front-row seat to Malia's journey. We loved her. She got new shirts to cover her growing belly. We all witnessed her morning sickness and cravings. During her pregnancy, Malia and I shared a bed. One of the funniest moments was when I was sleeping too close to Malia's belly, and my baby cousin kicked me.

Malia and I read the Bible together every night and looked for names to name her baby in the long biblical genealogy. Malia's baby was the first baby I'd ever witnessed being born. Only two people could be in the room, so opening the door quietly and checking the progress became my position throughout the night. Seeing her dilation was incredible. The miraculous way God made women's bodies was astounding to me.

Firsthand, I witnessed how hard it was to be a single teenage mother while trying to go to school.

When would she have time to work and provide for her child while going to school?

Malia was one of the strongest people I knew. My advice to her was to respect her mom and ask for guidance from Mrs. Jackson, who lived up the street from my auntie when Malia moved back home.

Unfortunately, the pressure Malia experienced is what people describe as "a baby raising a baby." Often painful to witness and feeling helpless in helping her on her new journey, I began a new journey of my own.

Speech and Debate

Besides seeing the birth of my baby cousin, the only positive part of my freshman year in high school was joining the speech and debate team. It was the only class available during seventh period after I dropped out of band.

My teacher was a short, happy, red-haired woman whose eyes sparkled when she taught. Some people laugh from their soul, and Ms. P certainly did. In my classroom were some of the best orators in the state. Not knowing this initially, I instantly knew because when they spoke, everyone sat up straighter in their chairs and leaned into what they were saying.

I was intrigued. People were taught to speak? Who would've known! I made fast friends with my classmates, even though I was one of the youngest. Often, they would talk about the immature and obnoxious freshman, but then reassure me, "Not you, Stephanie. You're the exception."

Seeing the debate team was impressive; however, my interest was more in giving speeches. My first speech was ten minutes on the topic of abstinence. After researching, writing, and memorizing my speech, I performed it all over the state at speech and debate events. My intentions were good yet misguided. Seeing my baby cousin born was life-changing and beautiful, and I also saw how near impossible it was to be a teenage mother.

My intention was to warn people of the dangers of engaging in sex as a teenager and the possible consequences. The words were true yet not transparent. I was too cowardly to expose my own shortcomings. A little more time would reveal even I lacked the conviction to live up to the standards taught to me by my parents.

My heart was critical and judgmental. Understanding and compassion for people with different values about abstinence eluded me. In the end, what came out was a self-righteous rant. The speech wasn't well received and came off more opinion-based with no real, practical, or tangible help for others, including myself.

Not acknowledging my own actions just a few years prior made the speech more egregious. The speech was an act of fake morality and superiority, shrouded in fear and a lack of transparency. In refusing to see myself in my peers, I remained blind. My ability to talk about the problems of our generation with my peers fell flat because my vantage point was too narrow.

Still confined in shame, I threw other people's faults into the light and became Pharisaical. In John 8:1–11, the Pharisees threw a woman who was caught in the act of adultery at the feet of Jesus so they could administer capital punishment: stoning.

Instead, Jesus told them, "Whoever is without sin cast the first stone."

What I find the most interesting about this story is that the people who put their stones down first were the oldest individuals in the group.

Believing I fully understood all the things high schoolers could experience developed an arrogance within me. My ego convinced me I knew more than I did. Recently, Jonathan, Celeste, and I were discussing why, at age twenty-five, it seemed like the light had finally turned on and we understood a lot more about life.

My response was, "We all tested out our theories about life and found out everything was a lot more complicated than we thought. Most the things we were so sure about we ended up being wrong about!"

Warren Wiersbe, an internationally known Bible teacher, author, and conference speaker, in his book *On Being a Leader for God* said, "Truth without love is brutality, and love without truth is hypocrisy."

This quote summarizes the error I was making in writing and delivering my speech on abstinence. Yes, some of what I shared was true; however, there was a lack of love. My speech carried a judgmental tone because I was judgmental of myself; therefore I was judgmental of others. If someone would have asked me, I would've said I loved people, yet I wasn't transparent or vulnerable about my truth, so I walked in hypocrisy. Before long, all my words were tested, and I found out why we are admonished not to judge or we will be judged (Matthew 7:1).

No Guidance

At age fifteen, my vision for my life was to be a young bride, possibly getting married in college. I imagined myself in a good marriage, convinced I could at least give and receive love, acceptance, and encouragement. College out of state seemed like the route to go. After getting my master's degree, my goal was to start a nonprofit helping homeless people in the city. Then the plan was to buy our first home together at age twenty-five, then we would start our family at age twenty-eight. Why? Because that seemed like a good age.

For having such a clear vision for my life at age fifteen, I lacked pertinent information to have healthy, romantic relationships. It was detrimental for my parents not to talk about sex, relationships, and dating with my brothers and me. If we would've asked, my parents would've talked to us and told us the truth; however, we never asked. Although my parents never lied to us, the simple fact that they didn't initiate these conversations made these topics feel taboo. Guilt, shame, and the secrets I held weighed my heart down.

Recently, guilt and shame was defined for me, and I want to share what I learned here. Guilt is an emotion felt when someone does something wrong, which is a healthy emotion when the guilt is felt, released, and the result is changed behavior. Whereas shame is an emotion causing the person carrying it to feel they have become inherently bad because of mistakes they've made. This was me. Shame overwhelmed my psyche all the time.

After various experiences, it became difficult to exercise self-control in my dating relationships. And with every indiscretion, my self-hatred grew. Unfortunately, in my childhood I met young girls and boys who were introduced to similar games (like house) when they were children too. In mutual lust, there were times we knew right from wrong and played similar games.

A group of us from church discussed the times our innocence was taken, and the seeds of destructive behavior planted in each of us. Even in those settings I didn't disclose all my secrets. For the first time, though, I did speak of experimenting with a girl when we were younger. I'll never forget, saying, "I can't do this anymore." And I didn't. There was no attraction, care, or love, only lust. Just as the pleasure was fleeting, the shame stayed. This conversation, although helpful, didn't heal me. I'm not sure it healed them either. Over time, as we grew older, we still made more poor choices in our sexuality. We confided in one another yet did not confide in anyone who could help us. None of us were courageous enough to speak to an adult about what happened to us, or what we were currently involved in.

At church camp, all we ever heard was that it was a sin to have sex before marriage, so don't do it. My parents told me the same thing. Talks about sex and purity were as deep as leafing through a pamphlet by oneself. Blatant and subtle messages from church taught us why we should continue to loathe ourselves.

In honesty, these messages weren't intentional or malicious. And still, one of the first indications a person is broken is their inability to hear clearly. The messages we all heard never provided a way out of our predicaments. A minister once said, "Sin doesn't shrink over time; it just gets exponentially bigger." I found that to be true.

Sadly, I heard more about dating, sex, and relationships from my friends at school, secular music, sitcoms, and my friend's *Cosmopolitan* magazine collection than from my parents, my youth group, church, or Sunday school. No one talked about trauma, abuse, or doing everything wrong before or after knowing Christ.

No one talked about what it was like to be impure. No one talked about how to forgive yourself for violating others, or how to forgive others who had violated you. No adults I knew spoke to people like my peers or me about theses hurtful and shameful experiences. In isolation, I began to feel like my friends, and I were the only ones with a past, or problems as heavy as ours. Instead of gaining the knowledge needed, I continued to struggle alone. Carrying secrets crushed me for years to come. In this mindset of lacking love for myself, I sought love from outside myself.

Looking for Love

Sophomore year was more peaceful, and I was less angry. Understanding the ebbs and flows of school made it less stressful; plus, everything at home was a lot more settled. Taking accountability for making myself miserable the year before by expecting everything to stay the same helped me to choose to be happy, make new friends, work hard, be less stressed, and to enjoy sophomore year.

I soon developed a fun friendship with a guy in my speech and debate class. Luke said and did things to irritate me, and sometimes to hear my thoughts. On various subjects, I often found myself shaking my head at him and his antics. Other times I would engage in his foolery. My teacher and our class-mates thought we should do a speech piece together because they said we argued like cats and dogs, so it would be a good dynamic. We laughed it off.

One day, Luke brought his cousin Kahlil to a speech competition. Luke had mentioned his cousin before; however, when we met, I was shocked. Kahlil was handsome. He seemed cool yet distracted as he focused on filling out paperwork.

"How old do you think Kahlil is?" Luke asked as I watched his cousin write.

"I don't know. Maybe a junior?" I said, raising my eyebrows at Luke.

"I'm filling out college applications," Kahlil said, looking up from his papers. "I'm a senior."

Smiling back, I shrugged. It was a guess, after all.

The following week at school while sitting in class with Katie, we talked about her current boyfriend.

"Katie, your boyfriend is a jerk. You should date someone else."

I could tell Luke was ear hustling. I smirked at him, then turned back to Katie. "As a matter of fact, Luke has a cute cousin. What about him?" I gave her a general description of what he looked like, not even knowing if Luke's cousin was single.

Luke laughed and said, "Oh yeah, my cousin said you were cute. And that's a good thing because he doesn't say many girls are."

I was surprised.

"Sounds like *you* should date him," Katie said. We both laughed.

"Well, he's coming to my house this weekend," Luke added. "We'll call you when he comes over."

Luke gave his cousin my phone number, and we ended up talking for hours over the weekend.

"Want to go to the movies in a couple of weeks?" Kahlil asked before we got off the phone.

I agreed.

The weekend we went to the movies there was a miscommunication, and Luke and Kahlil were at a different theater. We ended up waiting for hours, and my friend Shane, who was waiting with us, became hot. He sat up on a display case in the mall where a merchant had already closed their shop for the day.

As soon as Luke and Kahlil showed up, Shane let them have it. They both looked at him in disbelief. Kahlil didn't say a word; he looked at Shane and then looked at me. I was speechless.

Luke, being a charismatic people person, said, "My bad, man," followed by a quick apology to try and save the rest of the evening.

Shane spoke his mind and then had to catch the last bus home, so he hopped off the display case, gave me a hug, mean-mugged Luke and Kahlil, and he left. Katie and I sighed. Later, Katie and I debriefed on the chaotic night and had a good laugh at Shane.

A few days later, Kahlil and I were talking on the phone.

Talking about the confrontation, he said, "I thought your friend was going to try and fight Luke and me. I was a little concerned until he hopped off the display case."

I paused, unsure what he was getting at.

"When he was on the display case, we were eye level," Kahlil continued, "but when he hopped down, I had to drop my whole head to see him. I was like, this kid is like five feet tall."

I gasped. Kahlil and I laughed so hard tears filled my eyes. I shook my head. What a first impression.

Weeks later, Kahlil asked me to be his girlfriend and our relationship began.

8

Young Love

KAHLIL WAS IN HIS senior year of high school and preparing for college. He was planning on going to CU Boulder and had big dreams for himself. On the weekends, he would go to classes teaching students and their parents about financial aid and FAFSA. After telling Kahlil my aspirations for college, he helped me set up a personal email and my FAFSA account. We went to different high schools, so we always talked a lot after school. He began trying to convince me to go to CU Boulder, but I declined. Never knowing anyone who graduated from there was a deterrent, not to mention it was expensive. Going to college for free was my goal.

Dating

On the weekends, we passed our time together by studying or hanging out. One weekend I taught Kahlil how to play spades and dominos. It was fun until he started winning every game! At first, everything was going well. Then one day when we were on the phone, Kahlil called me a bi---. I hung up the phone before he could finish his sentence. Derogatory speech was extremely offensive to me. I was shocked. We weren't in a disagreement or an argument. The conversation we were having wasn't provoked and didn't warrant disrespect.

We didn't talk for a couple of days, and after a week or so I called him.

"Hey, I think we should break up," I said as soon as he picked up. I could hear him breathing deeply.

"Are you sure?" he said after a long pause.

"Yes, I'm sure." Immediately, sadness and relief filled me.

Looking back, I think my decision was hasty. What I truly wanted was to be with him, but not at the expense of being treated badly. Lacking the confidence to hold and communicate my standards to him was detrimental. Even after breaking up, Kahlil and I still talked all the time and hung out together. At this point in our relationship, we were exclusive even though we'd "broken up."

Natelie began dating my friend Luke, so every other weekend Kahlil and I would hang out with them. None of us owned a car so we walked everywhere. We would walk to the park, to the mall, to Natelie's house, or to Luke and Kahlil's church for youth group.

Our churches were different denominations. What I was taught was truth and what he was taught was truth were not the same. Being very adamant and arrogant about my beliefs wasn't helpful. He was studying and searching to know more. In my pride and immaturity, this became a division between us.

Despite our differences, we still did our best to be there for one another. On Kahlil's eighteenth birthday, my first greeting to him that morning was, "Happy birthday!" His birthday celebration was at his aunt's house. He was graduating in a couple of weeks, and he asked me to go to prom with him.

On the day of prom, Kahlil's stepmom took pictures of us. His dad refused to meet me. My feelings were hurt. I didn't understand why he disliked me when he'd never met me. We left and ate dinner at his friend's house. His friend's mother kindly made his friend group dinner.

At his prom, I felt awkward because I couldn't dance; instead, I passed the time watching Kahlil dance and laughing at his moves. While on the dance floor, one of the classmates he'd dated in the past walked by and pinched his butt. He laughed it off. I felt disrespected. Anger set in.

Later, Khalil said, "She thought you and I broke up, so what was the big deal?"

"Would you have liked it if someone did that to me!" I snapped.

The phone was silent.

To add insult to injury, when we got our prom photos back, his dad said, "She's not pretty. She looks like Celie from *The Color Purple*.

My thoughts raced. *Why would Kahlil's dad say something so hurtful to his son about me? His dad doesn't even know me. Why doesn't he like me?*

After Kahlil graduated, the summer passed quickly. Kahlil and I spent most the summer together, while I worked and performed with my drill team.

The Crowning of the Queen was a fundraiser where we asked people to donate money to our team to help with the cost of the program and travel. Whoever raised the most money for the team became the queen of the Colorado Starlites. That year, I decided to compete. First, I wrote a heartfelt letter about the character lessons and some of my experiences while being a part of the Starlites. I made a display board and pasted photos from two of our trips to California.

In my running for the crowning of the queen, my friends and family received letters in the mail while others were hand delivered. Mustering up the courage to ask the managers at grocery stores if I could set up a booth at the front of the store to elicit donations was no small task, yet my desire was greater than my fear of asking. As the end of the contest neared, my nerves took over because there might be a chance I raised the most money and would win. This was a huge night for me.

Waiting for the crowning to begin was nerve-racking. Kahlil sat next to me. Before long, he began complaining, asking when the event would be over. He muttered he had other places he needed to be. He was talking about his softball game. Irritated and disappointed, regret in inviting him filled me.

My thoughts raced. *Doesn't he know this was a huge deal for me? I should have just walked with my dad or one of my brothers.*

Our relationship was beginning to make less and less sense to me. Looking down at my hand confused me more. A few months back, Kahlil bought me a promise ring. He said he planned to write something meaningful to me before he gave it to me, but I was too nosey.

So what happened was it was my birthday, and Kahlil and I were on the phone while he walked around the mall. He asked, "What do you want for your birthday?"

Excitedly, I said, "I want a beta fish!"

He grumbled. "Seriously? You want a dumb fish? What else might you want?"

I couldn't think of anything.

Kahlil came down from Boulder to visit me on my birthday. It was during the week, so his effort was appreciated.

After he gave me my fish, he told me how he found it. "I walked out of a store in the mall and looked to the side, and there was a stupid beta fish kiosk. I rolled my eyes and bought you your fish."

I was beaming as he laughed at me. We sat talking and laughing about my fish. Happiness filled the room. As we sat there, he began shuffling through his bag nervously.

"What's going on?" I asked.

"It's nothing," he muttered.

Playfully, I pressed the issue. "No, what's in your bag."

Kahlil gave me a sigh before rolling his eyes and saying, "Whatever, just look."

As I looked through the compartments of his bag, I saw the ring. Floored, a ring was the last thing I expected. Looking at him sheepishly, he shook his head at me.

Kahlil was smart, handsome, and funny. I wanted to be with him long term; I just wasn't sure how we could fulfill one another's needs and have healthier disagreements. All these thoughts ran through my mind the evening of the Crowning of the Queen.

Eventually, we walked the stage and waited in anticipation. The host began calling the runners-up. I held my breath.

"The first runner up is . . . Stephanie Murray!"

Cheering sounded out. Amazement and sadness washed over me. For a split second, I wondered what the difference was between the winner and me. At the end of the day, though, I was happy to have contributed to my team, who had given so much to me.

I was presented with a trophy, and we took tons of pictures before my parents, Kahlil and I headed to a restaurant to celebrate. Mrs. Page gave me a hug, kissed my cheek, and congratulated me.

She said, "I have a gift for you. I'll get it to you at your next practice."

Kahlil and I began walking to his car so we could meet my parents. He felt inclined to add insult to injury. "First runner up is also known as first-place loser."

I took a deep breath. His comment was a jab. I wondered why he never seemed to know how to support and comfort me. He didn't want to be there, so he hurried in front of me.

The following week I went to practice, and Mrs. Page gave me my gift. "Make sure you're with a man who walks besides you, not way out in front of you," she said firmly.

I looked her in the eyes, then quickly looked down at my feet. I understood what she meant. Standing there, I wondered, *How can I communicate to Kahlil my desires without starting an argument?* Instead of asking the questions I so desperately needed answers to, I settled for a, "Thank you, Mrs. Page," then headed to church. The seed of what Mrs. Page said stayed with me for years.

Closer Proximity

The summer after Kahlil's first year in college, he began living with his aunt and working at a gas station up the street from my house. He was in transition, deciding if he was going to go back to college or if he was going to start working. Right before my senior year in high school, Kahlil bought his first car and began picking me up after school.

I was leaving art class and laughing with a classmate when I saw Kahlil waiting for me in the hall. I was so happy to see him. When we got in the car he seemed angry and asked me about my classmate. I didn't know why he was upset. I told him what we were talking about, hoping he'd drop it. Weeks later, I was getting ready to leave school and went to my locker to get my stuff. Kahlil went with me.

A different classmate named Al made a joke, and I simply laughed and grabbed my stuff.

Kahlil was furious. As soon as the car door closed, he said, "Really? You were all up in that guy's face smiling right in front me?"

I was shocked but tried to reassure him. "I wasn't smiling at him. I was laughing at what he was saying."

I didn't understand his outrage and insecurity because I was with him, and he was clearly better looking than Al. We got in an argument and didn't talk the rest of the day.

The following day I asked Katie, "Can you take me home after school?"

"Yeah, no problem," she replied.

Once I got home, Kahlil called me. "Where are you?"

I looked at my phone, confused. "I'm at home."

"I came to get you," he said through clenched teeth. I sighed, waiting for round two of our argument to start. It didn't until a few days later on the phone.

"Kahlil, will you take me to the store to cash my check?"

"Yeah, be ready at five. That's when I get off."

After cashing my check, he took twenty dollars out of my hand.

"Give it back," I asked.

"You're a stingy bitch!" he snapped back.

Immediately, I began weeping.

"I would've given you the money in a couple of days! It's rude for you to take the money out of my hand. And you're wrong for calling me out of my name! You know I'm on my way to take my senior pictures, and I need to pay the photographer."

He pulled up to my house, and I got out of the car and quickly slammed the door behind me. It was almost time to take my pictures. With encouragement from my friend Candice, I gave myself a pep talk so I could manage my emotions. Somehow, I needed to smile for my pictures. Frustrated, I wondered, *Why do we keep having these explosive arguments?*

In the following weeks, my parents hosted my birthday party at our house. A lot of my friends from school came. I got the prettiest flowers, gifts, and balloons. My mom cooked a spread, and some of my family came to visit. We laughed, ate, and talked for a while. Kahlil arrived late, his car window was damaged, and he was in a bad mood. He came by for a little while before quickly peeling off and leaving.

I decided I wasn't going to allow him to ruin the rest of my day. I wasn't even sure why he had come. I went back in the house and hung out with my family and friends. It seemed every time I needed support, or it was a time of celebration, his attitude affected my special moments, and ultimately our relationship.

Lost Confidence

Although Kahlil and I talked about marriage, our relationship concerned me. We weren't solid enough to transition into marriage. There were a lot of issues we needed to come to an understanding on and we hadn't. Whether it was religion or where I was going to college or how to solve conflicts in a respectful way, we were not on the same page. Over time, after Kahlil went back to college, another topic came up that we weren't on the same page about anymore: sex.

In earlier months, Kahlil told me he no longer wanted to continue the relationship if I wanted to wait to have sex. We'd been together for years and hadn't slept together, although our physical intimacy levels increased every year. We'd done everything besides having sex, and I was beginning to get nervous about it. I said I wanted to get married before having sex because that's what I was taught to do. My actions worked against my word and the standards I said I held for myself.

Unsure of what to do, we argued about how forward he was being. Still hoping we would eventually get married, I compromised. I didn't believe our relationship could take another point of contention. I was nervous, and the experience wasn't what I expected; it wasn't special. Regretting no longer being a virgin, I cried when I got home.

PART 3

LOSING LOVE

9

Not Finding Love

ONE AFTERNOON AFTER SCHOOL, my brothers and I were sitting on the couch in Andrew's room when I broke the news to them. "I'm pregnant," I said quietly.

I told Jonathan and Andrew first because they were closer to me than anyone else, and I needed some advice on how to tell our parents. Both my brothers were stunned. Jonathan rested his hand up to his chin pondering what I'd shared.

Out of my peripheral view, I saw a single tear roll down Andrew's face.

Jonathan broke the silence. "When are you going to tell Mom and Dad?"

"I don't know," I admitted. "I'm trying to figure out the right time to tell them."

Both my brothers looked at me in disbelief before Jonathan said matter-of-factly, "There's never going to be a perfect time to tell them. You just need to tell them."

Andrew nodded in agreement.

"You're right," I said reluctantly. "I'll tell them on Sunday."

I wrote a letter and read it to my parents the following Sunday. The only piece of content I recall from the letter is promising I would still go to college and graduate. My parents were sad and concerned, although they didn't have much to say in the moment.

Physician, Heal Thyself

Weeks prior to my pregnancy, I was selected to be a part of a student-led group who would be trained to support and counsel other students who were in crisis. The group was led by our high school counseling team. My classmate was presenting on teenage pregnancy. I shifted in my seat. At the end of the presentation, they began to go around the circle, asking our thoughts or how we would help someone who came to us and shared they were pregnant.

My secret was sitting right at the top of my throat. When it was my turn to speak, I said, "I'm pregnant. I told my parents last week. They are disappointed in me. I broke up with my child's father, and I'm not sure what my future holds."

My peers were sympathetic, and some even cried with me. Not one of my peers who sat in the room with me told my secret.

My personal high school student counselor was one of the leaders in the group and a phenomenal woman. After I shared, Ms. E didn't discourage me; instead, she sent me every scholarship I was eligible for. I never felt she didn't believe I could still accomplish my dreams. She was kind, supportive, and nonjudgmental. There were times I didn't know what to do, and she shared parts of her life she thought might help me.

"Have you ever thought of adoption?" Ms. E asked.

I shook my head no.

"Adoption was a gift for my family and me," she added.

Ms. E shared her family's experience with adoption.

I listened intently before replying, "I can't imagine adoption for myself because I'm having a child with someone I loved. Also, I don't think I could do it after feeling my baby kick inside me and seeing them on the ultrasound."

Patiently, she offered hope and advice without making me feel pressured or misunderstood.

Early the following week, I told Katie, "I have something to tell you. Can we go to lunch?"

As we sat in her car I spoke honestly. "I went to Planned Parenthood with Kahlil."

Katie knew we were not in a good space in our relationship. We were in between breaking up and staying together over the last year, and nothing was improving. Things were just getting worse.

"Kahlil and I got in an argument, and we didn't talk for a couple of weeks. Then in February, my period didn't come. I texted Kahlil and told him I thought I was pregnant. So last week we went to the clinic."

Katie looked at me, obviously concerned.

"Kahlil picked me up after school so we could go to the clinic. We walked in the door, and I filled out the paperwork. We sat there in silence. I went back and took the pregnancy test. The nurse confirmed I was pregnant. I took my paperwork and walked out of the examination room. As soon as I saw Kahlil in the waiting area, he asked, 'Are you pregnant?' I nodded my head. We went out to his car. 'What are you going to do?' he asked. I wasn't following him at first. I was still stunned from the news. Kahlil's second question broke through the silence when he asked, 'Are you going to get an abortion?' I was shocked. In between my tears I said, 'No, our baby doesn't deserve to die. It didn't ask to be here. We brought it here.' Kahlil went on to say, 'Hey, I'm dating Carol, and I'm going to be with her.'"

I wept silently. I was speechless. I hadn't even finished high school yet. I was applying for scholarships with my friends Linda, Jen, and D, taking final exams, and filing out college applications to start college in the fall. In between school, I worked at the same retail store Natelie worked at. I made only $7.25 an hour. This was no condition to have a child in.

As I sat there processing it all, I solidified in my mind our relationship is over this time.

I was talking to Katie, but more to myself, "Why was I the only one committed to our relationship? Why am I still wearing this ring he gave me?"

Katie looked at me in bewilderment, going from anger to sympathy. "If I were pregnant and my baby had a heartbeat, I wouldn't have an abortion either." I nodded tearfully. "I'm here for you, Stephanie." And she was, consistently from sixth grade until now.

I was reluctant to tell my best friend Natelie I was pregnant though. A few months prior a mutual friend of ours, Logan, saw Kahlil was dating another woman.

Logan was driving Jonathan and me to school when she asked, "Are you still with Kahlil? He was being pretty friendly with Tori. It looks like they are together. Does that seem like boyfriend behavior to you, Stephanie? Seems like something you should look into. Right, Jon?"

Jonathan nodded his head and looked out the window of the car. I did too. I was embarrassed and hurt she brought this up in front of my brother. My lack of self-esteem was starting to become apparent to those closest to me, and they didn't understand it. The previous summer Natelie, Logan, and I got into a disagreement because they were tired of seeing me defend my relationship with Kahlil. To them, it appeared to have run its course.

I worked in the misses department, and it was a wreck. While I cleaned, thoughts swirled around in my head and began raining down on me. *What did I need for my baby and for myself? Am I going to have a boy or a girl? In art class, I painted*

Spiderman in case I had a son. I need to choose a name, but what should I name my baby? And where will we live?

Natelie worked in the home department. After she finished her tasks, she decided to come over to my department to help me.

"So how's it going?" she asked casually.

Eventually, I told her I was pregnant. Natelie wasn't shocked, so I knew she already knew. *Who told her?* I thought. She gently asked a few more questions. I was relieved she seemed empathetic.

A few days later, Natelie told me her ex-boyfriend, my friend Luke, told her. I was annoyed and at the same time knew I needed to get over it. It was time to muster up the courage to tell my extended family.

You're Not the First

Grandma Murray would often come and stay at my family's house for weeks at a time. We looked out for her, and she would look out for us. There was one particular day I was having a hard time with my pregnancy. Morning sickness set in, all my doctor appointments began, and I was overwhelmed. I was crying in the family room as my mom was talking to me.

My grandma came in with a furrowed brow and asked, "Stephanie, what is it? What's wrong?"

I didn't want to tell her. All her other granddaughters were married before they had children. I was disappointed in myself, and I thought she would be disappointed too. My mom looked at me in a reassuring way to share my truth and to be brave.

"I'm pregnant," I answered.

Her response shocked me. "Well, you're not the first woman to get pregnant, and you won't be the last." She patted my hand and chuckled.

I tried to give her a smile. I wasn't sad about having a baby. I wanted to have children eventually, just at age twenty-eight, not at nineteen. And not with someone I wasn't married to, and especially not with someone who didn't love me.

My family began to connect with a few families in our church. One of the families were the Thompsons. Sister Jay was newly converted and brought her sister, Dawn, and mother, Janice, into the faith. I came to love them all. Sister Dawn's temperament was like mine, and I easily connected with her. She was real, godly, kind, and funny, so I came to trust her.

At church one day Sister Dawn asked, "How are you wearing your hair for prom?"

I had no idea. We talked on the phone a couple of times, and she got excited. Sister Dawn planned for us to meet up at the hair store to get supplies on Saturday. While she ran into the store, I sat in the car with Sister Janice, and we talked for a while.

We had a simple conversation that changed my life. I talked to Sister Janice about all the good things I could think of, and eventually I shared with her what was on my heart every second of every day.

"Sister Janice, I'm pregnant, and I don't know what I'm going to do about going to college, childcare, my finances, or how I'm going to get along with my child's father."

She looked at me before stating, "You can still go to college. You can still do everything you planned on doing before you got pregnant. The only one who can stop you is you!"

I nodded my head. She'd encouraged me and reminded me I still had a future if I didn't get stuck in fear and instead chose to keep moving forward.

In the evening while I got my hair done, Sister Dawn said, "Stephanie, never be ashamed of your testimony. Sometimes we fall. Just know we have to get back up. God has got you, and we got you too!" They did, and they still do.

Second Prom

On prom night, I got ready at Linda and D's house before we meet up with Jen at the venue. We took tons of pictures, danced, ate, and went to Boondocks to play until the wee hours of the morning. We enjoyed ourselves. Two of our friends were crowned prom king and queen. It was a perfect night.

Weeks before, I saw my name on the royal ball nominees voting sheet. I was shocked. I wouldn't describe myself as popular. I wasn't at the house parties, nor did I date any of the popular guys. Yet I was still on the list.

Generally, I was kind and friendly, besides freshman year when I kept to myself. When it came to school, I was driven and studied hard. Being in my step team the Colorado Starlites, having a job, being inducted into the NHS, participating in speech and debate, volunteering, and being a writer for the newspaper kept me busy.

I was selected for the student counseling program because of my consistent nature, trustworthiness, and loyalty. I was awarded multiple scholarships, which included attending a conference and being given a computer from a local rotary club.

For senior favorites I was voted "Most Likely to Succeed" and "Best Dressed." Being on the nomination sheet for the prom ball along with the other acknowledgements and awards surprised me. There was a stark difference in how I saw myself and how my peers perceived me.

I mention all these things because although I was authentically being me, I felt like an imposter who somehow fooled everyone around me. All the accomplishments and accolades didn't improve the lack of love I carried for myself. I hated myself and lacked self-esteem. I wanted Kahlil and others to do for me what I had not done for myself: to love, value, and choose me unconditionally.

10

Love's Reality

IT WAS SENIOR WEEK, and every day Katie and I would go to various senior class activities together. We went to get our caps and gowns and yearbooks. Our last week we went to lunch, took pictures with our friends, joked, and laughed in the halls or signed one another's yearbooks. One of my best memories was going on our senior camping trip.

The End of a Season

I almost got Katie's car stuck on the way up. Thankfully, one of our guy friends knew how to navigate the terrain better, so he drove the rest of the way. It was a beautiful place. The first time I ever slept on the ground in a tent I was pregnant! What was I thinking? However, I enjoyed the time laughing, talking, and watching my friend Linda dance by the fire. We set up our tent and huddled together because it was so cold. I wasn't sure how much my life was going to change in the coming months. All I knew was that I was committed to celebrating life as it was through the end of my senior year.

During the last few months before I graduated from high school, I was never home. If I wasn't at school or with friends, I was at work or church. In the months leading to graduation, Kahlil showed up at my house multiple times unannounced.

I was always gone. My mom would tell me he came by. I wondered what he wanted. I never called though. I just focused on finishing high school strong. I didn't want to deal with any drama. I needed to focus on saving money, finishing my finals, and planning my graduation party.

High school ended, and summer began. My pregnancy was a secret the last four months of my high school career. It was difficult to tell Linda, one of my closest friends, I was pregnant. We studied together, applied for scholarships, got to know one another's families, and were even partners for multiple projects. Linda was reserved yet caring.

"I'm thinking about taking a semester off of college in the fall," I said casually.

When she looked at me, her eyes watered, as if I could hear her pleading with me before she said any words. "Please, don't take a semester off. So many women have said they were going to take a semester off and never went back."

I wasn't completely committed to the idea of taking a semester off, so my ears and heart were open to listen to her advice. I nodded my head and decided right then and there I would begin college in the fall.

After high school graduation, everything slowed down. Kahlil and I met up. We hung out a couple of times. I never asked him why he was back. I was unsure of his motives. It was awkward. For two people who talked every day for years, we were struggling to even exchange small talk. One day he came to my job, and we took a walk on my break. We shook our heads, looking at my growing stomach.

"Hey, why didn't you invite me to your graduation party?" he asked.

I looked at him, puzzled. "We haven't spoken in months. Why would I think you would come to my graduation party? You told me you were dating Carol?"

As he looked down, shuffling his feet, he asked, "So what else have you been up to?"

"Senior week, camping, working, finals, senior award ceremonies, prom."

He looked shocked when he found out I'd gone to prom and wore the same dress I wore to his prom. Although we had just begun speaking again, I gave him his ring back. Trusting him again terrified me. Finally, I was settling into my nightmare of not being with him. I'd fortified my heart despite his reentrance into my life. It just wasn't the same, and I wasn't sure it ever would be.

Summer 2006

My friend Luke, Kahlil's cousin who introduced us, was in an awkward position in both our lives. I was at home when Luke pulled up in his truck.

He sauntered up the driveway and asked, "Hey, Stephanie, do you and your brother want to go to Dairy Queen?"

Jonathan and I stood in line with Luke at the ice cream parlor, trying to decide what we wanted. Luke looked up at the menu and said, "Hey guys, it's my treat. Get whatever you want."

We ordered and sat down inside, then Luke broke the silence. "I feel sorry for you, considering this whole situation."

Unbeknownst to him, Luke disclosed to me for the first time, "It's crazy that Carol is pregnant too. Kahlil is so angry; he and Carol broke up."

I was stunned. I felt betrayed because Kahlil hadn't told me. Now all his recent behavior made sense. The rest of our visit was a blur. My thoughts became a roller coaster, climbing, turning, screeching, and lurching before flying down the tracks of my mind. Any spark of hope of reconciliation had been suffocated.

Communication with Kahlil was nonexistent at the beginning of my pregnancy and had recently resumed again before I was told this information. He was never at any doctor's appointments. Nurses asked me questions about Kahlil, and I gave no answers. I felt their stares, impatience, and disdain for me. I was a pregnant teenager.

Not being able to openly talk to the person who was directly a part of this new experience about the scary, exciting, and interesting developments of this new life only reinforced my feelings of abandonment that I carried with me. We hadn't eaten a meal together, bought clothes for our baby, or chosen a name. I began processing what reality was and what I'd always hoped it would've been. My reality choked me up at the most inopportune times, like standing in the grocery store checkout line.

The year was 2006. My first child was due, and it felt as if every celebrity was pregnant. Strange situations can enhance feelings of loneliness. While l stood in the line at the grocery store, I saw a plethora of beautiful pictures of women expecting children and their spouses or significant others standing there with them in joy and what appeared to be love. How I longed for my experience to be as joyful as theirs. Up until that point, I'd fought for any joy I had, yet I wasn't joyful at all now. I was in sorrow.

I waited a day before I called to confront him. I called Natelie first. I borrowed my mom's car after dropping her off at work. I was as sad, as I was angry. Tears poured down my face. I told Natelie what happened. She listened to me and asked a couple of questions. I could hear the anger in her voice.

Katie was in Texas, so I called her too. She consoled me by saying repeatedly, "I'm so sorry, Stephanie. I'm so sorry."

The next day at work I couldn't hold it in anymore. I was walking around like a zombie. I couldn't even force a smile or muster up a laugh. I was in the break room alone, so I called. He didn't answer. His phone went to voicemail.

After the beep I said, "You're a lying, deceiving bastard, and I want nothing to do with you. I hope you'll be there for our daughter." I hung up the phone and threw it in my work locker.

A few weeks prior, I went with my mom and Natelie to have an ultrasound. I wanted to have a boy, thinking that relating to a boy would be easier, having four brothers and all. My brothers and dad said I was having a boy. I'm not going to lie; after the ultrasound, I was disappointed for a couple of hours when I found out I was having a girl. I sat on my bed at home with Natelie, trying to think of names for a girl, and came up with Amorisa. I combined the word *love* in Spanish and my mom's name, Risa. So together her name meant love and laughter. It was beautiful. I began telling everyone I was having a girl.

I was placed with an in-home nurse who helped teenage moms. She helped me a great deal by normalizing all the changes happening in my life. She connected me with another teenage mother who became my friend. Her story was similar to mine, and she'd overcome major adversity. The first day I met Zahara and her family, we went to lunch together. I was shocked when she and her family blessed me with a personal baby shower. They gave me clothes for my daughter and a beautiful cake. They were some of the most loving people I'd ever met.

My friend Logan gave me the book *What to Expect When You're Expecting*. I began reading it in between my shifts at work. When the store manager saw I was pregnant, he put me on the cash register the remainder of my pregnancy. I got countless compliments of how I glowed. How people felt happier after I helped them check out. Getting hit on multiple times a week was strange though. The men always apologized once they recognized my round baby belly.

I'm thankful for positive interactions because soon enough I was going to see what some people thought of unwed teenage mothers. One day I came into the manager's office who put me on a register to hand in some paperwork when the he cheerfully said, "Hi, fatso."

I cut my eyes at him. He shifted in his chair, and I made sure he felt uncomfortable with my gaze before I said, "Actually, it's a baby!" I turned and left the office.

I was furious, and still nothing could compare to the comment a coworker of mine said when she found out I was abandoned by my child's father.

She casually said, "Oh, so your baby's a bastard?"

I could've punched her in the face.

Instead, I said, "No, I have my dad and four brothers who will surround her." I imagined a little girl in the center of a circle made up of my dad, Jonathan, Andrew, Matthew, and Josiah.

The ultrasound technicians, doctors, and nurses I saw on a regular basis where very short with me. Whenever I asked questions, they didn't seem engaged or concerned. I felt like they answered me with a disciplinary tone: "Well yeah, that's what happens when you're pregnant."

One day I was with my parents, and we were picking up a few things from the store. We ran into a family friend we'd previously gone to church with.

When she saw my baby bump, she said, "Oh, I thought you actually served God."

My eyes dropped along with my heart. I remembered a conversation we had years prior when I expressed why I believed in God and how I was trying my best to follow him. I shared with her a few reasons why I believed, like my cousin being saved and my mom recovering from severe depression. Me getting pregnant didn't automatically make me a liar and what I shared untrue.

I wanted to say, *I tried hard to do the right thing. I can assure you, I let myself down, I let my family down, I let God down. I don't need your judgmental words. I'm already judging myself.* But I didn't. I saw my dad's smile quickly fade, hung my head, and walked away. I was not concerned about explaining myself, nor did I have the energy for a cordial good-bye.

Relationship Change with My Parents

While I was growing up, I was always closer to my dad because he talked more and always asked great questions. Ninety-nine percent of the time I was with my dad, we laughed. When I got pregnant, I felt I had deeply hurt my dad and that he was disappointed in my choices. Our relationship took a hit. We weren't as close. Being the helpful man my dad is, he would go to the store for me, or go sit with me in the social services offices. He even told me I should go to the annual church conferences because the messages I missed would've helped me. He helped me to identify how I felt when it came to being rejected and abandoned.

Although my relationship with my dad was strained, my relationship with my mom was established. My mom was there for me in a way I'd never experienced before then. I realized that one of the greatest gifts my mom possesses is her strength and stability for people when they are down. She was in my corner, there for the hurting underdog, me. I felt truly loved and accepted by my mom when I didn't meet her expectations, which was a new and strange experience for me.

My mom was kind to me. Sometimes we worked out together to an exercise video. She built and painted a changing table for my daughter and personalized it with her name, Amorisa. She attended key appointments and a birthing class with me, yet one of my fondest memories was when we watched a PBS special called *The Miracle of Life.* It was so amazingly beautiful to see the miracle of life begin from attraction until birth. The film made us cry. Becoming a mom connected me to my own mom.

Love Your Neighbor as You Love Yourself

My high school counselor gave me a recommendation to go to counseling. I called and set up an appointment with the family counselor who visited with my mom and me at the school a few months back. I began going to counseling once a week the remainder of my pregnancy.

At my first visit the family counselor asked for one or both of my parents to come. My dad was working, so my mom came in. We sat in my newly assigned counselor's office together, then she began asking us a few questions to get to know us. Then, in an unassuming moment, my mom shared her story.

"Stephanie, your dad and I found out I was pregnant with you two months into our marriage. Now I did want to be a mother one day. However, I wasn't mentally or emotionally ready to become a mother so soon."

She took a deep breath and went on. "One day I cried and cried all day long. Now I know, I was overwhelmed with fear, anxiety, and stress about being a new wife, managing an apartment complex with your dad, moving to a new city, and being pregnant. Unfortunately, I didn't understand all these emotions back then. My negative emotions turned into anger, and I began punching myself in the stomach. I thought perhaps I would have a miscarriage."

Her tears began to flow, and mine did too.

Through her tears she said, "About a week later I was listening to a Christian broadcast, *Focus on the Family*, and they shared a story about abortion. I was deeply impacted by the story. On the broadcast, I heard the woman in the story carried guilt and shame and how she experienced God's forgiveness. This truthful story is what began the healing process for me too. I realized Jesus not only forgave me, he loved me and trusted me to have children.

My mindset shifted. Children are a precious gift from the Lord. I felt convicted and sorrowful for what I did in my anger. I asked God to forgive me. I never told your dad what happened until many years later, and now I'm sharing this with you. That day in the counselor's office, I considered what my mom shared. I never asked any questions.

Years later, when I heard my mom's full story, I realized this incident became just one more painful part of her life that she had kept to herself. One hurtful or painful experience after another she carried along with her into the next season of her life.

In recent years my mom said, "I feel like what I did to you when you were in utero wounded you. Perhaps you struggled with your identity, self-image, self-esteem and self-love because of what you perceived when you were in my womb. I'm sorry, Stephanie. I pray you heal and can forgive me."

Considering who my mom was and how desperately she was struggling in hurt, shame, and insecurities, all I have for my mom is compassion and forgiveness. We can only love others as we love ourselves. How difficult it must have been for her to realize she wasn't ready emotionally, spiritually, and mentally to be a mother even though she desired to be one. Her actions reflected her fear.

My mom had not yet experienced how the Lord doesn't give us a spirit of fear; He gives us a spirit of power, love, and a sound mind. I have never made right decisions out of fear, and it's with this knowledge and understanding I chose to forgive my mom. She was on her own journey alongside me. No, she didn't get everything right, and neither have (nor will) I.

All I know is my mom became a loving, forgiving, resilient, beautiful, God-fearing woman who overcame, and I'm proud of her. I love her. Jesus chose her womb for me, and for the moment it was unsafe, He held she and me until the storm passed and she was no longer sinking. She chose to steady her gaze on Jesus. Each of us can learn from her; there is forgiveness and healing when we fall. Repent and run to Jesus. He'll remind you who He is and who you are, a loving light, obliterating all fear.

Decisions

As my body began to change, I began thinking about what my parents told me years before: "How a woman feels emotionally while she is carrying a baby is important." I understood that if I was happy and at peace, my baby would be too. But if I was angry, bitter, and stressed out, my baby would be too. So once I told the people I chose to about my pregnancy, I worked on being as happy and at peace as possible.

Natelie was excited, and I got excited to. While we were at work, we started looking for baby clothes and items I could buy to furnish my first apartment once I got it. I saved money and waited for sales so I could get as many items as I needed for my baby. I still didn't work many hours, so it was hard saving money. I applied for Medicaid and food stamps so I could at least save money on food. Countless times, Natelie would invite me to go eat dinner with her and she'd treat me. We began calling her my "baby daddy." When people heard it, they looked bewildered, and our chuckle would turn into a loud laugh. It was nice to laugh again.

11

Birthing Love

ABOUT A MONTH BEFORE I gave birth, my counselor said, "I think you are doing better, and you now have some tools to help you in the next chapters of your life. How do you feel? Do you feel like we need to continue to meet?"

I just agreed with her. She was the expert, after all.

The End of Our Sessions

In a moment, my counseling sessions ended. Regrettably, there was a lack of self-assessment; therefore I didn't advocate for myself. My lack of self-awareness, vulnerability, and transparency prevented me from getting the help I needed. I was too busy attempting to appear good that I wasn't willing to do the work to bring about healing and wholeness. I just wanted to be better, even if it meant faking it.

I hated feeling broken, abandoned, rejected, embarrassed, and ashamed. In error, I believed that because the counselor said I was "doing better," she was saying I had processed the entire mental, emotional, and relational trauma of my experiences. Counseling helped me, yet I didn't fully understand how vital it was for me to have a specific time every two weeks dedicated to processing my past and present to have hope for the future.

A Midterm Birth

The last few months of my pregnancy, I began talking to my baby. "I need you to come on Friday so I can finish my midterms, okay? Can you help me with that?"

I would say, "We're going to be okay! We're going to succeed! We're going to have a great first semester in college!"

The week before my due date, while on the phone with Katie, we discussed all the last-minute things I needed to get done before going to the hospital. Two tests were scheduled for the same week I was due. My nerves were high.

In confidence I told Katie, "I'm going to have my baby on your birthday, next Friday, October twentieth."

Katie was so excited she told her boyfriend. "Stephanie said she's going to have her baby on my birthday!"

"That's dumb," he replied. "I don't know why she told you that. She doesn't know when her baby is coming."

On my due date, October 17, I went to my friend Annette's house to get my hair braided. As I sat in the chair at her house, she asked, "Girl, when are you due?"

"Today," I said casually.

"What are you doing here?!" she exclaimed.

"I'm going to have my baby on Friday," I assured her, laughing.

Thursday after my last midterm I headed home. I was exhausted. When I got nervous, I kept telling myself, *There are billions of people on the planet, and they were all birthed. I am a woman, and my body was created with the ability to give birth.*

8:33 a.m.

It was 5:00 in the morning, and I began to feel discomfort in my lower abdomen. I woke up to the sharp pain and the sound of my parents closing the front door of the house. They were both leaving for work. I was at home with my two youngest brothers, Matthew and Josiah. Jonathan and Andrew had spent the night at their friend's house they had a football game that evening. I tried to go back to sleep and couldn't.

My mom told me the cramps I got while on my period were nothing compared to contractions, so I assessed my pain. This pain was about as bad as my cramps, so I decided to begin my laboring process at home. First, I drew myself bath. I sat in the bath for a short while, but then it began to hurt too much to sit. So I stood up and started a shower. I stood there for a few minutes before the pain became too unbearable, then I turned the shower off and went back to my room.

I laid down and the pain intensified, so I called Natelie at 6:00. I made myself wait until six because I didn't want to wake her up too early. With it being my first birth, who knew how long it was going to be. I heard it could last anywhere between eight to twenty-four hours. Being in labor for twenty-four hours sounded dreadful. I hoped my labor would be closer to eight hours.

Natelie answered on the first ring. "Are you ready?"

"Yes," I replied.

I got dressed and woke up my two youngest brothers.

"Matthew and Josiah, can you pack a hospital bag for me?" I proceeded to give them instructions in between my contractions.

I know, I know. For someone who knew when their baby was coming, seems like I would've packed my hospital bags prior, right? Well, I didn't!

And when Natelie got there, she shook her head at me and called our friend Logan.

"Okay, I'm going to jump in the shower and I'll be there soon," Logan replied.

I went into the bathroom and I began heaving. After I went to the restroom, I realized my water broke and there was a green tint in my amniotic fluid.

When I read *What to Expect When You're Expecting*, it said if you saw green in the amniotic fluid, your baby was under stress. As soon as I caught my breath I said, "Natelie, call 911!"

To make sure she heard me right through the bathroom door, she verified what I'd said: "Call 911?"

"Yes."

She called them and talked to the operator. I was so annoyed. *Were they coming or not?* From the questions they were instructing her to ask me, it seemed they were assessing whether they needed to come or not. I wasn't aware they were on their way, and the questions were just their protocol. I sat in the rocking chair in the front room of my house.

The EMTs came in casually. They put me on the gurney and lifted me into the back of the ambulance. Natelie and Logan jumped in the car to meet us. One handsome EMT was singing and joking with his coworker. He was so calm and happy, and it irritated me.

To time my contractions he said, "Tell me when your contractions start and stop."

He chitchatted with his coworker and timed my contractions in between their stories.

"Your baby is going to be coming very soon!" he informed me.

I rolled my eyes, thinking, *How do you know? You're so busy talking and laughing!*

The EMT driver began asking how to get to the hospital I was going to because he'd never been there! I frustratingly told the driver how to get there in between my contractions.

Once we got there, I saw Natelie and Logan, who said in unison, "You should have driven with us! We beat the ambulance here!"

I mustered a smile and shook my head. When I got changed into the hospital gown, I went to the bathroom; it felt like my whole body was contracting like an accordion.

Siting on the bed Natelie said, "Do you want me to rub your back like they showed us in the birthing class?"

I declined. "No thanks." I didn't want anyone to touch me.

The nurse came in and I asked for an epidural.

"I'm not sure. We have to check to see how far you're dilated." She checked me and said, "You can't have an epidural because it time for you to push."

Natelie, Logan, and I looked at each other in shock. It was just going to be us. I was sad for a moment because I knew my mom wanted to be there, and I wanted her to be there too. The nurses got prepared, and I began pushing. The doctor barely made it by the time I gave my last push.

Logan stood at my head and reassured me. "You're doing good. Your baby is almost here." Her voice was so soothing and comforting. With her always joking, playing sports, and being a smart aleck, I'd never witnessed this nurturing side of her. I'm not even sure she knew this side of her existed, and yet it was beautiful.

Natelie was holding my left leg in true baby daddy form. Watching the birth and supporting me, she made a couple of comments, and Logan leaned down to see. Then Natelie pushed her back because Logan was squeamish of blood, and we didn't want her to pass out.

On my final push at 8:33 a.m., they lifted my baby and set *him* on my chest. We all gasped. My baby was a boy!

"O my God! It's a boy," I exclaimed. The nurses looked at us strangely.

"I was told I was having a girl," I said, confused.

We all looked at each other, crying and laughing.

Immediately, I thought about my family. My dad dreamed of me having a boy, and my brothers were convinced I was going to have a boy. They didn't accept the ultrasound technician's analysis at all. At work, I was a cashier, and over the last several months my growing belly often became a subject of conversation. People would always ask me what I was having, and I would proudly tell them I was having a girl. The older Hispanic women and some of my coworkers would look at me puzzled and say, "No, you're actually a boy shape." I would just smile. After all, what did I know about a boy shape?

I called Katie.

As soon as she answered I blurted out, "I had my baby. It's a boy!" followed by "Happy birthday!" We both laughed, and I gave her a quick synopsis of what happened. She was just as shocked as we were about how quick my birth was and about me carrying around a boy. I called my parents to tell them. They were so excited and began heading to the hospital.

Then I thought, *What am I going to name him?* I decided to call my cousin Malia. When she was pregnant years back, she and I chose a boy's name she hadn't used because she gave birth to a girl. I called to ask her if I could use the name. She agreed, as long as I told him how his name was chosen. I named my son Eli'el, which means, "he is God's, and God is his."

Eventually, it became quiet, and Natelie asked me what I needed from my house. After Natelie, Logan, and I made a plan, I asked, "Did you see the EMT?"

They looked at me and laughed, They already knew what I was going to say: "He was fine."

When I saw their shocked faces, I said, "Just because I was in labor doesn't mean I couldn't see!"

When my parents came in the door, they were both beaming. My dad kissed me on the forehead and told me he was proud of me. My mom was excited to hold Eli'el. They smiled so big in every picture we took.

My brothers came in after their game, smiling and laughing. "I knew you were going to have a boy! I never believed what the doctors said, ultrasound or not!"

My brothers came with their familiy the Brotts' and Natelie's parents. Natelie's parents bought gifts for my surprise son and me. The next day, my friend Maria, from my drill team, and her husband came to visit after Katie's mom, Judy, and her sister Sarah came to visit with a huge bag of baby clothes. I was overwhelmed with gratitude.

In the evening I experienced an uncomfortable conversation with the nurse. I needed to decide whether or not I wanted my son's father to sign his birth certificate. I hadn't spoken to Kahlil since I left the voicemail on his phone several months back. I texted him and told him we had a son. I invited him to come see him and sign the birth certificate.

He agreed to come. It was strange. He came into the room and immediately started looking at everything in the room, inspecting it and asking questions. I'd never seen this side of him. He was cordial, and I was too. He held our son, who looked identical to him.

Leaving the Hospital

Sunday afternoon we were discharged, and from there it was off to the races. Choices I'd made brought parenthood nine years sooner than I'd planned. I was ready to leave the hospital, so the doctors discharged my son and me. Right after the nurses ensured the car seat was properly installed in my car, I thought, *Really? You're just going to let me leave now, after two days? I don't know what I'm doing. I've never done this before, and now I'm pretty much on my own. I need to keep an extremely small person I created alive?*

There was a lot of learning and growing for me to do. In the hospital, I began to realize the daunting journey ahead after I was informed I needed to learn how to breastfeed, and part of learning was to teach my son how to suck. Who would have known you have to teach a baby to suck? I sure didn't. I looked at Natelie in bewilderment. Thank God she was able to explain to me what the lactation nurse was saying.

12

Love Is True

IN THE MONTHS AFTER my son was born, I felt scared and shaken. Originally, I'd planned to move away and attend college at an HBCU. Instead, I stayed at home with my family. I not only felt guilty having a child at this stage in my life; my family was struggling financially, and I felt I was adding to the strain.

In the summer, my family was evicted. Immediately, we began packing feverishly. After moving in with Grandma Murray, our family was at one of its lowest points. No one knew what the future held. My grandma was gracious to let us move in; however, there wasn't enough room for ten people in a two-bedroom, one-bath home. My son and I slept in the front bedroom, Grandma slept in the den, and my parents took the tiny bedroom in the back of the house. My brothers slept on the floor under the dining room table and on couches. In the fall, they had to get up at 5:00 a.m. to have time to navigate the city buses to school.

We were all miserable. Frustrations and resentments ran high. It was chaotic and hard for everyone. The good news was that I was with my family. The bad news was everyone was in crisis.

One day I heard my grandma on the phone complaining about all of us. I was shocked. I had never heard her say anything negative or hurtful about any of us before. My heart dropped as I wept quietly. This situation was less than ideal, and I needed to get my son and myself out of there.

One day I told Katie, "I have to find a new job and place to stay."

What she said next came as a wonderful surprise. "You know, Stephanie, my parents are really busy in their painting business, and they would be willing to hire you."

I had been working part time in retail making seven dollars an hour. I quickly gave two weeks' notice and accepted a job offer from Katie's parents, Judy and Frank.

I was going to make three dollars more an hour and would have steady work and maybe even get bonuses!

Two Weeks

Early each morning I would get the address of the job site and show up to work. After two weeks, Katie's parents knew it wasn't going to be a good fit. On Saturday, Judy called me, crying.

"Stephanie, I'm so sorry, but you're not catching on quick enough. It isn't your fault. It's so busy that we can't train you right now, so well have to let you go."

Shocked, I began to cry.

"Can you go back to my previous employer?"

"No, I can't."

The next morning, Judy called me back and told me she and Frank had come up with a plan. "You can help me in the office for the same wages. When you're not working, make a resume and apply for jobs the rest of the day."

I couldn't believe my ears. All I could muster was, "Thanks, Judy. Please tell Frank I said thank you too."

The following Monday I began working in the office. Sometimes I would help paint trim for various houses, but most of the time I helped Judy. In about a month I got an interview at a bank, and they hired me!

Eli'el and I had moved out of my grandmother's home and were staying with my aunt—but it was a temporary fix at best.

One day Katie said, "You know, my sister and I moved out of our parents' house and their basement is open. Maybe they would let Eli'el and you move in with them."

Judy and Frank agreed to let Eli'el and I move in rent-free so I could save money and get on my feet. Their home was nice, and Eli'el and I were comfortable there. Judy was kind and considerate. She often purchased things my son or I needed without me asking. Frank and Judy included us in nightly dinners and on family holidays. They even allowed me to borrow money for car repairs, helped me job search, and gave me the best advice they could.

Not living with my family opened my eyes. While living with Frank and Judy, I saw a couple who worked extremely hard owning a business together. Taking time out to enjoy recreational activities was equally important to them. Witnessing financial stability and their generosity was very impactful. Hearing Frank play the piano and watching Judy writing poetry, biking, or cooking became great memories. Over the year and a half we stayed with them, we became a part of their family, as I continued in college and began a career in banking.

My Network

The first two years of Eli'el's life, Kahlil and I fought to find common ground and trust. Kahlil and I were young and immature. We did our best to care for and love one another, yet we hurt one another and, ultimately, chose to not be a couple. This was the first mature decision we made. In time, Kahlil and Carol married. We learned how to communicate and compromise, and we overcame our differences, hurt, and pain. We forgave because we loved Eli'el. To this day, respect and love is all I have for Kahlil and Carol because of all we have overcome together.

My family provided the perfect balance. They were willing to help me care for Eli'el when they could, or when they were in between jobs. I would pay them, and as soon as they got steady employment, they would inform me I needed to find different arrangements. My brothers, my parents, my friends, and at times my grandmothers would watch Eli'el while I went to school and work. They were willing to help yet not willing to hurt their future in order to help me, and I'm glad they didn't. Over time, unbalanced sacrifices could have bred resentment.

At one point in time, my son was taken care of by a friend's mother. It was a good setup at first, but I couldn't afford what she was worth, so I got on day care assistance with the state. My son entered traditional day care. I hated it. He was constantly getting colds, bitten, or scratched. And their pick-up times were often when I was getting off work. If he wasn't picked up on the dot by who I coordinated pick up with, I got charged fees.

Taking care of my son on my own was hard even with an extensive, intricate network of family and friends who supported Eli'el and me. I felt like a burden by depending on them, but not because of them. It was my own intrinsic desire to be independent. The thought of relying too heavily on my family when they had their own life and struggles bothered me.

In the midst of my single motherhood journey, I was often driving over forty miles a day between transporting my son to and from daycare while going to school full time and working full time. In my busyness, I established a destructive habit of not taking care of my spiritual, physical, emotional, and mental well-being.

Even though on the surface it looked like I was doing okay—working a better job, taking classes, and going to church while surrounded by supportive family and friends—the truth was that I was a twenty-year-old single mom drowning in hurt, pain, and confusion while trying to embrace a life I didn't know anything about.

Healed

Every month I participated in family prayer meetings. There were about five families from my church who would come together to have a potluck and pray together. We would work through problems together. Family prayer meetings helped me to feel supported and learn how to be transparent about my struggles. The environment caused me to seek out help in order to move forward with sure footing for my son and me.

One day in our prayer meeting my dad said, "Stephanie, I had a vision of you. You were going on a trip. I see you attempting to move forward, but you're dragging a huge, old, tattered suitcase behind you. God's telling me that's your past. Now you need to have the courage to let it go. Can you do this for me? Will you make the motion of throwing the old suitcase away from you?"

I cried as I swung my arm and unclutched my fingers, symbolizing letting go of my past.

I wish I could tell you I didn't pick up the weight of my tattered past again. I did leave it for a while. Unfortunately,

I picked it up again because it was familiar baggage. When my son was young, going to prayer meetings and counseling appointments was a part of my routine. In error, I stopped doing the things that I knew brought wholeness to my life. Lacking these components in my life hurt my full recovery.

Jonathan and I have discussed having great success in our lives, and once we arrived at a place that was our vision of success in a particular area, we stopped the daily tasks or practices that got us there—all while expecting to stay and improve in those same areas. Foolish, I know. And that's the lie complacency tells all its victims.

Somehow, we don't have to continue doing the small habits until they become a lifestyle. We believed in a place called *there*. Time passing deceived me into believing I'd learned all the lessons from the traumatic events and situations that changed the shape of my life, when in reality I hadn't started or even finished some of the internal work. After being single for two years, I turned twenty-one.

At twenty-one I thought I knew the difference between a man who was good, faithful, loving, and understanding and one who was not. I wholeheartedly believed I'd learned all I could from my previous failed relationships.

My perception was I'd learned far more than I had. Therefore what I thought I learned and what I actually learned was not the same. First, I learned some people lie. Second, I understood being a single parent is rewarding and requires double the sacrifice when only one parent is involved full time. This season in life showed me everything my son or I knew was because someone taught us. And the last truth I began to grasp was that life could be completely different than I'd planned. However, I could still reach my goals with God, support, and a desire.

Most the time I blamed Kahlil for the woes in my life. Instead of dissecting the choices of my past, I skimmed the surface of them. I believed the biggest mistakes I made was trusting the wrong people. Blaming didn't allow me to see myself for who I was. Furthermore, a blaming mindset didn't allow me to adequately take responsibility for my poor choices or acknowledge how I thought and felt. And my subsequent actions kept me from becoming the young woman I believed God called me to be.

When I was a child, I prayed and asked God for a gift He promised His believers. It was the infilling of the Holy Spirit, given for the first time to believers detailed in Acts 2. At the time, the one thing I wanted most, besides the Holy Spirit, was a Murray bike. I thought it would be amazing to have my last name decaled on my bike.

I went up to the altar and told God, "I want the Holy Spirit more than I want a Murray bike."

I repented for any wrong I did and said, "Thank You, Jesus, for dying for me. Thank You for my family and my friends."

My lips began to quiver, and tears rolled down my cheeks. Suddenly, I experienced my first memorable supernatural experience when I spoke in a language I was never taught. I felt warmth, and I can only describe it as a beam of light. I felt at peace and was infused with incredible joy. Later that evening I was baptized, and I felt that my soul was cleansed.

Then when I was twelve, I was given an open vision of a transitional housing facility I believed God was calling me to open. I even saw my husband in the vision. Who I was at age twenty-one and the woman I needed to become to fulfill the vision I saw from God were two different women, and I knew it. I questioned whether my mistakes disqualified me from the work I believed wholeheartedly God called me to do, especially since I wasn't married.

I knew I wanted to be a wife and have a family. Either of those desires weren't bad in and of themselves. What was wrong was what I believed these relationships would bring me. I desired to be a wife because I wanted to love and be loved unconditionally. I wanted desperately to be completely known, understood, safe, accepted, and appreciated. I didn't want to be single; to me, singleness represented loneliness, abandonment, and rejection. I thought being a wife and a mother made me worthy of my calling.

Did I consciously know this? No, yet my soul and my subconscious knew. My false perception was that I was happy, confident, and content. Underneath the masks I was insecure, fearful, had low self-esteem, and did the right things in order to be accepted and approved of. I was so engrossed in the day-to-day tasks of life that I wasn't aware of my personhood. The tasks were important and necessary, and still I didn't know the greater importance of continued self-care and internal soul work.

I was in a training at work when I heard former Defense Secretary Donald Rumsfeld say in a briefing on February 12, 2002, "There are known knowns; there are things we know we know. We also know there are known unknowns; that is to say we know there are some things we do not know. But there are also unknown unknowns—the ones we don't know we don't know."

I've found those are the blind spots in life and often cause the most destruction. In that season, I was preoccupied and unaware of my spiritual, mental, physical and emotional health. And what I didn't know I didn't know turned out to open the door to one of my greatest falls.

PART 4

COUNTERFEIT LOVE

13

Lust

NATELIE, CHRISSY, AND I were seated at a table, waiting for our food, when a man walked in to pick up his to-go order. He looked familiar. We met each other's eyes a few times, yet I couldn't place where I had seen him before.

"Who's that?" Natelie asked.

"I know him. I just don't know how."

I kept thinking about him. It took weeks to realize who he was.

Drawn In

In my junior year of high school, I had just arrived at the community rec center for step practice when I noticed a man staring at me with such intensity I thought he was looking at something behind me. When I realized he was staring at me, I hurried away, flattered and confused.

After practice was over, he approached me. As we chatted, he said, "So do you have a number?"

"I do, but I have a boyfriend," I said quickly.

"I respect that," he replied. "Well, nice to meet you."

Nothing else was ever said as I gave a small wave and bolted up the stairs of the rec center.

When I figured it out, I explained it to Natelie. "I figured out who the guy from the restaurant was. He's a boxer I met briefly at the rec center several years ago."

I couldn't deny I was attracted to him.

Months later, I stopped by my grandma's house, and there he was again in front of the rec center where he trained across the street from her house.

I was lifting Eli'el out of his car seat when I heard someone say, "When did you have a baby?"

"A year and some months ago."

"Where's your boyfriend?" he asked.

I raised my eyebrow and smirked. "I don't have one."

"A bet . . . Let me get your number then."

In the age-old saying, the rest was history.

On one of our first dates, Chance told me over the years he'd told people we were going to be together. He even said he'd prayed for me. I was skeptical. I wasn't sure if he was running game.

One day I was dropping him off at home and met his uncle.

Chance introduced me and asked his uncle, "Unc, do you remember the woman I told you about before? The one I said I prayed for?"

"Oh yeah, I remember," his uncle responded. "Nice to meet you."

It was then I believed him. This was before I understood some people may even use their uncles as wingmen. Once I believed him, I felt desired and appreciated. I was relieved someone cared enough to pray for and about me.

These may seem like simple pleasantries; however, I had been humiliated and rejected by the fathers of my last two serious boyfriends. They hadn't known me and thus told their sons they didn't like me. Both of their fathers also said I wasn't pretty. And one of the fathers told their son he should see what else was out there.

This time felt different. Chance seemed to want to be with me. And a bonus was that Chance's family seemed to be accepting as well.

I was wooed by words. I've loved words most of my life. My mom read to us as children, and my fifth-grade teacher, Mrs. P, inspired me to read books on my own. From that time on, I was hooked on words and stories. My naivety prevented me from knowing that people tell stories too. Some stories are fictional, presented as nonfictional tales.

Time hadn't yet afforded me the wisdom to know I needed to intently watch one's actions before opening my heart to someone's story, goals, dreams, or aspirations. Why? Because unknowingly one can choose to become a character in the storyteller's life. I was enchanted with what seemed like honest words. Chance's words told me I was desired and accepted. They said I was enough, and I soaked it all up because I was like a parched wetland in the dry season.

Have you ever seen a wetland in the dry season? The lack of rain has left it cracked and completely depleted. If any water hits it besides torrential rainfall, it will look as if it had never been watered. Unless the wetland is completely immersed for days, the effect of the rain would never be realized in such a dry place.

My heart looked like a wetland in a dry season. I didn't know the torrential rain of fully being chosen, accepted, and loved could only come from God. People didn't have the ability to make the dry land of my heart a flourishing wetland, no matter how good they were or appeared to be.

Falling Fast

From our first date on Chance and I were inseparable. Phone calls, text messages, dates, and intimate information was shared quickly. This was the work it took for me to trust him; for me to give all of myself. After our first date, I called Chance mine. Natelie looked at me warily. She was happy for me yet shocked at how fast I was connecting with him.

Quickly, I become caught up in the moment, in the idea, in the distraction, in my desire to be in a relationship. A sixteen-wheeler going eighty miles an hour down a dark, winding road with no headlights on is how I'd describe my blind headlong pursuit of the relationship.

Katie's father, Frank, said, "Take your time."

Instead of asking him directly what he meant, I simply said, "Okay."

Instead of listening, I justified my decision by saying, "This is a second chance for Chance and me. Previously, he had pursued a relationship with me, but it just wasn't the right time because I was dating someone else. Now is the right time!"

In hindsight, I realize Frank told me to take my time because I became a single mother just two years before. I was told I was loved before, then I was abandoned and left to nurture a child alone. My life was just starting, however, the odds were stacked against me because of my choices.

Now, I know Frank wanted me to observe my pursuer's character before I fell madly in love with his words. Taking my time meant not to get emotionally and physically intimate with him based on what he said. I heard what Frank said. I didn't listen or understand his words though.

Compromising

Chance just became a pro boxer, and his first debut fight was coming up. He was busy training and sparing. I was busy taking care of my son, going to school, and working. Even though we were busy, whenever we could be together, we were. We went to lunch, watched movies, laughed throughout the day, and introduced one another to new dinner spots. We spent our birthdays together and exchanged various gifts throughout the year. I was so comfortable with him, I felt like I'd known him for a long time.

It wasn't long before we slept together. I *fully* accepted him.

When I told Natelie, she gasped and said, "Stephanie?" She said my name in an almost scolding tone. Looking back, she was probably in shock and amazement, and had some possible concerns.

Opening up and being intimate with someone so quickly was unusual for me. Our connection was magnetizing, seductive, and caring. It was exciting, fun and even peaceful at times. Soon, Chance mentioned us moving in together.

"I'm not going to move in with someone I'm not married too," I said.

"Married? Huh, it's kind of soon to be talking about marriage. I know well be together though," Chance replied.

We began renting hotel rooms and staying the night together.

A couple of months prior, Chance's debut fight was in Las Vegas at the Hilton Hotel. We talked often, and I listened to and prayed for him. The day of the fight I was nervous all day at work. I scoured the internet to find updates and articles about the fighters. I waited patiently by the phone for hours to hear if he'd won.

Eventually, the call came. Through tears, he said, "I lost, babe. I lost." I couldn't believe what I was hearing. I cried. Immense regret flooded me, and I wished I was there with him. I felt sick to my stomach. I'd never heard him so low; he was devastated. So much of his hopes, dreams, and plans for our future were predicated on him winning that fight.

After we talked briefly, he left the hotel. I called him dozens of times. Natelie told me not to worry; he was probably walking to clear his head. She was right. A few days later I picked him up from the airport. He looked the saddest I'd ever seen him. We were happy to see each other, but I felt deeply how hurt he was. He was already talking about getting his next fight and needing to redeem his name. I sought to understand and encourage him the best I could.

Meeting the Family

A month later, Chance went with me to Grandma Murray's ninetieth birthday celebration week. I was excited for him to meet my family and all my cousins, especially my cousin Celeste.

A year earlier (when I wasn't dating anyone and was much more faithful in my spiritual walk), Celeste had texted me and said she dreamed Jesus was coming back, and she knew she wasn't living right. She'd then called me and asked, "Cousin, will you teach me how to pray?"

"Celeste, I've made a lot of mistakes. However, I will teach you what I know about prayer, and we can began doing Bible studies together."

We did, and some of her friends joined us too. Celeste and I became close.

Even though I wasn't walking with Jesus in the same way, I knew she loved me, and I was looking forward to seeing her again.

There was food, tears, laughter, stories, and lots of picture taking. My grandmother's house was filled to overflowing. As the festivities ended, we were all outside talking. My little cousin said something Chance thought was funny, so he laughed. He didn't know how horrible the actual situation was. Celeste was hurt and angry, so she proceeded to cuss him out. The misunderstanding happened so fast; I couldn't intervene fast enough. I felt sick to my stomach.

"He doesn't know what's going on!" I told Celeste.

She was furious, and he was in shock, then his face turned. His head cocked to the side as he said, "I'm not 'bouts to do anything. I got some female relatives though. Any of them can handle you."

I was appalled.

My cousin Jinnelle chimed in: "This is all love around here. You're going to have to take that somewhere else!"

Quickly, I told my cousins, "We're going to go."

My excitement quickly turned to disappointment and sadness. *How did a beautiful day turn so quickly?*

Never having witnessed this amount of anger from my cousin or Chance was confusing, and there I was in the middle.

We didn't talk much on the drive back. When we got to his house, we began to argue.

"What was all that about? My cousin was dead wrong. However, you threatening her was just as wrong!"

Chance saw nothing wrong with his behavior. I began realizing we were a part of two different worlds with two different rules of engagement. It seemed our relationship was going to end as fast as it began.

"Blood, she came at me," Chance began defending himself. "If she didn't want that reaction, she should have shut her mouth. I know some females who would have hit her dead in her mouth. She won't get a second chance with me."

He got out and slammed my car door.

Sunday came and at 10:00 a.m. our church service began.

Celeste came up and said, "Sorry, cousin, will you forgive me?"

I nodded. We shed a couple of tears and we embraced.

"Hey, my cousin apologized at church today," I told Chance later that day.

He mumbled some things under his breath about her not being tough. He seemed like he was going to let it go. I just wanted the situation to end.

Overall, my family is generally accepting and kind, so it was hard to gauge their feelings at first. My parents and most of my brothers seemed to be indifferent to Chance. They didn't know him well enough. Yet after the situation with my cousin, Jonathan made his opinions known.

"I was suspicious of him at first, and now I know I'm right. I don't like him. I keep seeing you cry around him, and I don't have the capacity to pretend I like him. I'm just letting you know."

14

Questioning Love

FRANK AND JUDY TOLD me they were selling their home and moving to their dream house in four months. I was happy for them.

"You and Eli'el can stay for the next six months while we get our new and old homes prepared to move into and to sell," Judy said at dinner.

Destiny Shifts: Warning Before Destruction

Brother Marquies, who is my brother from church, gave me a warning. "Don't allow your brothers or any other men to stay with you, sister. Just save money and get prepared to move."

Although I felt like I was getting closer to Chance, I felt like I was drifting away from my relationship with God. I didn't listen to God's warning from brother Marquies. Soon after Frank and Judy moved, Chance began staying the night with me regularly.

Months quickly passed, and my moving date was fast approaching. I bought all the furniture for my home and began setting up apartment tours on my days off. Soon I began comparing square footage, prices, locations, and amenities. Overall, even though Chance suggested it, I still lacked peace when it came to moving in with someone I wasn't married to.

A family friend told me about a nonprofit that provided housing, lifestyle classes, and childcare for single women and their children. The rent was reasonable, which attracted me too. Anxiety filled me while looking at other apartments because of the cost of rent and utilities.

I filled out the application, toured the property, and went through the interview process. The nonprofit said I was a great fit; however, the waitlist was six months.

One evening Chance said, "I can't see our relationship continuing if we don't move in together."

I repeated my conviction that I didn't want to live with someone unless we were married. Then I added with matter-of-fact confidence, "If you don't marry me, then someone else will."

He was shocked. I quickly saw that what I'd said had hurt him. The hurt I saw left his face as quickly as it was exposed. I wasn't sure what to say because I meant what I said.

Before I could respond, he said, "Never say that again."

Face-to-face, he reached out for me and reiterated, "Never say that again."

A few weeks later on a quiet afternoon, we were sitting on the couch watching a movie when he turned to look at me.

"Will you marry me?"

"Yes."

We began looking for apartments together.

A Growing Family

In the meantime, I was struggling with being a parent. I didn't know how to raise Eli'el, so I learned as I went.

Eli'el was wonderful child. He had dozens of facial expressions. I tried to capture them all in photos. He was very curious and expressive. He wanted to know why and how things worked. We read a lot of books together, and he liked animals, especially dogs. Something I noticed about my son was how he observed people and could articulate his thoughts and feelings intelligently. He thought deeply about things, and his questions went far deeper than surface rhetoric.

I did everything for him because I didn't know what else to do. This caused him to be spoiled. When he wouldn't listen, I was good at communicating right and wrong, yet at first I failed at knowing effective ways to correct him when he wouldn't listen.

I was even worse at enforcing consequences. I didn't know I did this until Chance pointed it out to me. Chance and Eli'el had a good relationship because he would play with him, reward him with small toys, and give him boundaries. He wasn't mean or overbearing. My inconsistency with discipline irritated Chance immensely, and it began countless arguments between us. Chance had four other children who lived with their mothers. He had been a parent longer than I had been, and I would've appreciated his insight with grace. Unfortunately, all I was met with was irritation and disgust from him.

I was also overwhelmed by the costs of raising a child. My son got sick often. His sicknesses were nothing out of the ordinary, but they were scary nonetheless for a first-time mother. Going to the ER and forking out one-hundred-dollar copays, being up with a sick child all night, and needing to turn in a term paper the next day were constant challenges. I didn't know how to get him into day care or into school, or how I would pay for all of his expenses until I walked through these experiences.

I was also still reeling from the shame I'd felt at becoming an unwed mother. I felt so much shame at the church I attended. When I was pregnant, I wasn't permitted to have my baby shower at the church because supposedly it would be showing other young people the church approved of unwed pregnancy.

There were also hurtful comments. One day someone who attended my church—someone I considered a friend—said, "When you got pregnant, I felt better about myself because I always put you on a pedestal in your walk with God."

When I mustered up the courage to go to church conferences, I heard so many voices in my head. I dreaded people talking behind my back, saying something cutting or judging me behind their stares. I imagined the parishioner's internal dialogues the most in an effort to protect myself and lessen the blow if someone ever approached me, or I heard someone was talking about me.

The voices were relentless: *Is that so-and-so's daughter? Didn't she grow up in the church? See, what you do in secret will come out in the light! Wow, now we have unwed teenage mothers in the church? What a shame!*

It's difficult to drive up to the church, walk into the door, raise your hands in praise, and worship while voices in your head are screaming at you. Sometimes I went anyway. I tried.

I was barely standing back up in life when I found out I was pregnant again.

This time, I didn't feel as brave as I'd felt the first time I got pregnant. I was no longer ignorant. I knew how people would talk about me. I knew the kind of sacrifice it would take.

And I believed I didn't have what it would take.

When I told Natelie, she said, "But you're in a better space. And in a better relationship, right? I wouldn't advise you getting an abortion."

Natelie knew me. She often reminded me of who I was when the lies I was listening to were too loud.

I wish would've listened to her.

Ring, Ring!

I called an abortion clinic.

The woman on the phone answered. "You have one of two options. We can give you a pill and your body will release the sac at home, or you can come in for a day procedure and we will remove the embryo by vacuuming your cervix."

Her matter-of-fact tone startled me.

"Neither of those sounds right to me."

My eyes filled with tears as I hung up. Another week passed. Fear was overwhelming me, and I couldn't escape the dozens of questions in my head:

What if my fiancé leaves me like my son's father did?

How will I be able to afford to care for two children on my own?

Will my family be angry with me this time? Will they help me with two kids when I need help?

How will this affect me finishing school?

I called Planned Parenthood again and set up an appointment. They told me how much it would cost. When we pulled up to the office, there were picketers out front. They began shouting at Chance and me.

"Don't kill your baby!"

Pictures of aborted babies were posted on their signs. They were adamant and passionate. I couldn't believe there were so many people outside the gate, shouting and holding up signs. There were men and women, both young and old.

We put the hoods of our jackets on, lowered our heads, and walked into the office. There were women sitting in chairs filling out paperwork. I sat and filled out mine. No one made eye contact. They took me into another room and did an ultrasound to confirm that I was pregnant.

They talked about the procedure again, and I lost it. I went into another room with a counselor and Chance. The more we spoke the more I realized I couldn't go through with the procedure.

When we left, the picketers were gone. I felt relived. When Chance and I ate lunch, we started talking about what we were going to do, and the relief I felt left. He voiced his fears of not being able to provide.

Once again, I was uncertain. Once again, I was overwhelmed with fear. *I'm going to be abandoned again. If I have to do this alone again, I will fail this time. I can't face what I faced before. It's hard having one child. What will I do when I have two by myself?*

A few days later I asked Chance to drive me back to the clinic.

I woke up in a dimly lit room. Someone told me to get dressed and handed me a prescription for pain.

I felt numb. I felt exhausted. I felt alone.

For weeks I experienced horrible cramping and bleeding, a painful reminder of the choice I had made.

One day I was so afraid I called the clinic back. The nurse was very matter-of-fact. She verified that I was experiencing the side effects of an abortion.

I went into a deep depression. I cried a lot. I ate a lot. I felt so guilty and ashamed. I began to fall apart. I wasn't sleeping well. I began struggling in school and at work.

Yellow Notebook Paper

It was a Saturday afternoon. I looked out the living room window and saw my dad and Jonathan walking up the driveway. I knew what prompted their visit. I had missed our family prayer meeting last week. In fact, I had been intentionally avoiding my family as I began going backward into my old lifestyle.

What I didn't know was that God had spoken to Jonathan about me.

I greeted them at the door and invited them into the living room where we sat on the couches. We didn't chitchat. In fact, the mood felt somber. I turned on the lamp as the sun started to go down.

My brother held a yellow lined piece of notebook paper in his hands.

"Stephanie, God spoke to me about you. I wrote down what he told me, and I want to read it to you."

I sat quietly, not saying a word. In fact, my emotions had completely shut down with grief, overwhelm, and depression. My family didn't know about the abortion four months ago. What's more, three days prior I had discovered I was pregnant again. I couldn't even process that news myself, much less share it with my family.

My brother began to read:

Stephanie, you have been walking in the position of a crown long before you knew that's what you were.

You have been crowning young men God hasn't told you to. He never will. You have placed yourself on the head of a man, but God didn't put you there.

You are like a child trying to build a castle out of sand. You have built men out of your own image and understanding, but they were not of God, so they crumbled underneath the weight of your crown.

Your crown is heavy and is supposed to be placed by God on a man made by God strong enough to bear it. Men you build out of sand will never stand forever. Only clay God has breathed life into will become the man worthy of your crown.

You have forgotten the promises and signs God has given you for encouragement; instead, you build sandmen according to your own thoughts and understanding.

God will give you to a man you never thought of. Take peace and comfort in the fact that God knows more than you and that God loves you more than you love yourself.

You think he chose you. The truth is, you accepted Him.

You think you're a crown, but really you're a trophy.

You think you're a crown, but you're a footstool.

You think you're walking in God's will, but the truth is, you're in the way.

You think you have to mold him into a man of God, but the truth is, God has to mold him.

You think you have to accept Him as he is, but the truth is, he's unacceptable.

You think you have to hold him up to God, but the truth is, he has to hold himself up.

You think all relationships have struggle, but the truth is, there's grace for the ones based in God.

You think you built you up, but God built you up, and he'll break you.

You think you know your worth, but you don't, and he doesn't either.

If you don't make a sacrifice, the angel will not pass over your house.

If you let yourself touch the ground, your kingdom will fall.

I listened intently to what my brother said. Although he was right, I didn't share what was in my heart. I didn't ask for help. I couldn't. I was too busy concealing the truth.

He leaned toward me and handed me the yellow-lined sheets of paper.

That night, I thought about the words on the pages as I set them on my nightstand.

I felt like crying, but I was too emotionally exhausted.

I finally fell asleep, my eyes dry and my heart broken.

15

Unlearned Lessons in Love

CHANCE SNAPPED AT ME every time I tried to pick up a box.

"Don't lift nothin' up," he scolded. "You're carrying my seed."

The Secret Is Out

My dad and my brothers helped Chance and me move into our new apartment. I was three months pregnant and had finally broken the news about the baby to my family. My family didn't agree with my decision to move in with Chance, and still they showed up to help us.

Within one week, things began falling apart.

"Chance," I said one morning over breakfast, "I got a letter from the child care assistance program. They need more paperwork to keep helping with Eli'el's child care, and we've just got two weeks to get it to them or we might be removed from the program."

"What do they need?"

"Since we signed the lease on the apartment together, they need proof of income from you."

Chance grunted, but a week later he had yet to produce the paperwork we needed.

When I asked him about it, he said matter-of-factly, "My pops said not to give you any paperwork. He said they don't need to be in my business."

I was furious. "Chance, the caseworker told me there's a waitlist. If we're dropped from the program now, it will be impossible to get two children in the program later."

He didn't budge.

How was I going to be able to afford daycare for my son and our new child? Why did his dad have so much say in our relationship and our household? After all, he wasn't contributing anything to our budget. Why didn't he care about the children being cared for?

A strange pattern began. Chance was hanging out with his friend a lot, who he called his "brother." I would often ask, "Do you want me to come and get you?"

"No, my bro will drop me off," he'd reply.

A few hours would pass, and he'd call me and say, "My bro got drunk. He can't drive me home, so I'm just going to stay here."

I began to feel like he wanted to move in together to keep tabs on me, not because he wanted to be with me.

When my cousin Jinnelle found out I had moved in with Chance, she said, "Cousin, you shouldn't move in with him." She recited a phrase from a revival we'd just attended together. "It's 11:59."

The phrase meant it was too late to go back and forth with God, and now my destiny was in the balance. I listened to her, yet my heart was hardened.

"I understand your concern, cousin, but everything will be okay," I replied.

Not What It Seems

I lost my day care benefits for my son, so Chance agreed to watch him while I was at school and work. When I returned, he would go to the gym so he could train. I appreciated him helping me, yet I was concerned he was going to begin blaming me for his inability to work during the day. He claimed he was working with his dad, who was starting a nonprofit.

The first month he paid his part of the rent, then every month thereafter, for over two years, he didn't pay any household expense. We were living on my extra scholarship money. I was frustrated because he wasn't keeping his word with paying his part of the bills, and we were barely making it. My car broke down, and I began catching the bus and light rail to work. At times, Jonathan would take me to work and drop off Eli'el at day care.

He and Chance never spoke. Chance mentioned it to me, and I asked Jonathan to say hello only to keep the peace for me. Every reason I decided to move in with him was proving to be an inaccurate portrayal of the truth he told me. Without knowing it, I began to lose respect for him because he never kept his word.

A few weeks passed and a float teller named Dominic came into work. He was shocked when he saw my growing belly. He was as charming as he was blunt.

"Why didn't you learn from your parents?" Dominic asked. "Weren't they married before they had children so they could establish a family for you?"

I felt like I had been punched in the stomach with shame, embarrassment, and guilt. He had just put words to one of the painful questions I asked myself every day yet didn't have the courage to answer for myself. I knew the answer would bring about a decision I didn't feel I was courageous enough to acknowledge or act upon.

Months later my heart was crushed. I got off work and walked into my grandmother's house to pick up my son. The phone rang and I answered. There was a woman on the phone who asked for me. I was puzzled. I didn't live at my grandmother's house, and I never gave her phone number out as a contact for me.

Right away, the woman asked, "Do you know Chance?"

"Yes," I replied.

"Did you know he has three kids and he's married?"

My heart sank and I felt physically sick. I looked down at my growing belly and began hyperventilating. I knew about his three children. But I didn't know his divorce proceedings weren't finalized.

Once I caught my breath, I replied, "Yes, he's never lied to me. He told me about his children, and he showed me his paperwork for his divorce. He's been honest with me."

She scoffed and said, "Good luck with that," then hung up the phone.

Crying, I called Chance several times before he answered. When I told him what had happened, he tried his best to calm me down.

"And how does she know where my grandma lives?" I asked, upset. "Or that I just walked in the door? And how does she know my grandma's phone number?"

"I'm sorry. She's just angry that we're happy and in a new relationship. It will be okay, babe."

"Is it true your divorce isn't finalized?" I asked angrily.

"Hey, I showed you the paperwork. I'm talking to a lawyer to look at a few pages. With losing the fight, I didn't have the rest of the money to pay him."

My crying turned into weeping. I hated myself.

How had I been so naïve and stupid? Why did I so easily believe men who said they loved me? When was his divorce going to go through?

I didn't have any of the answers to these questions, nor would I get answers. I was having another child in a worse situation than when I'd had my son.

I felt humiliated.

Our Baby

Chance and I began going to doctor's appointments, and I convinced him to let the gender of our child be a surprise. He reluctantly agreed.

We began sharing possible names for the new baby, but since we could never agree on anything we both liked, we put the decision on the back burner for a while.

In the meantime, I loved looking at the ultrasound photos and dreaming about the new addition to our family.

I was due in August.

This pregnancy was different. I was extremely fatigued and felt nauseous all day for months. A client at the bank told me about a natural supplement to help with my nausea; I picked it up from the store right away. I showed a lot faster than I did with my first pregnancy, and I was a lot bigger, craving Philly cheesesteaks, cake, and ice cream, which was unusual for me.

We were happy about my pregnancy, and both regretted our decision to get an abortion. It affected us more than we realized it would. We were both trying to get our peace back, and soon we began getting into our routine as a couple. Chance loved summers the most because I took time off from school. I didn't always have a book in my hand or a computer in my lap. We would go to the library and specialty ice cream parlors. We stayed up late watching movies, cooking, laughing, and talking.

Over the next several months, we came into a happy place. Chance was attentive and supportive. At times being at work stressed me out. After getting frustrated at work, I went home on my lunch break and he always hugged me. I felt cared for and safe. The months passed, and I couldn't wait to have our baby. I was growing immensely uncomfortable. I felt happy this time around with midwives who listened to my concerns and helped me write out a birthing plan.

I went into the hospital a week after my due date to induce labor. It didn't work; our child wasn't ready to come. The next morning I cried when I heard other babies being born in different rooms and I was being sent home. Another week passed and still no signs of birth, so they scheduled another induction. I'd really hoped to go into labor naturally like I did with Eli'el.

By then, I realized every pregnancy is different. My parents took care of Eli'el, and I headed to the hospital with Chance. We still hadn't decided on a name. They began giving me Pitocin. I didn't opt for an epidural because I didn't want to slow down my dilation. In the hospital, I thought of a few boys and girls names. I said them nonchalantly in an attempt to not sound too excited so maybe Chance would agree on one. My logic seemed to work. Finally, we agreed on baby names!

A few hours passed, and my mom had come directly from work to the hospital. She was determined not to miss out on this birth. After she went down to the cafeteria to get some food, my contractions became unbearable. As she came back into the room, the nurse was coming in to check on me.

"Can I have an epidural now?" I asked the nurse.

"Sorry, sweetheart. It's time for you to push."

I'd done it again! I missed the window to get an epidural.

This time, my mom held one of my legs, and Chance held the other. This was the first time my mom would witness a birth. At one moment during the delivery, my mom made a yikes face; it was so funny. If I hadn't been in immense pain, I would've laughed.

Chance was watching the midwives and nurses like a hawk. On my final push I said, "Oh, God!"

Looking down, I saw I'd given birth to a baby girl. We named her Kadiri, which means "mulberry tree" in Japanese and "capable" in Swahili. She was beautiful.

When we got home, our daughter was fussy, and I couldn't get her to go to sleep, so Chance lightly rocked her in his hands until they both fell asleep. I looked at them sleeping peacefully. I forgot how quickly infant babies need to be changed, but Chance reminded me. I got up in the middle of the night to feed her because I wasn't resting well with her lying beside us. I was paranoid Chance or I would roll onto her, so we put her in her crib.

Kadiri was a great baby. She ate well and slow, wanting to eat every half hour it seemed. I called her a snacker. At first, I was expecting her to eat like her brother, who I called the guzzler; instead, she took her time and never threw up. The first time I heard her scream it jarred Chance and me out of our sleep. We ran to her crib and discovered her teeth were coming in on the bottom. We looked at each other in disbelief; she was only four months old.

She hated baby food, so we mashed up food and fed it to her. She loved Eli'el and began trying to keep up with him. Chance taught her to wave her left fist if people got too close to her face. He loved it, and I just shook my head.

One time we were in the grocery store, and everyone was stopping to look at Kadiri.

"Why are they looking at my sister?" Eli'el said in his newly found protective voice.

I explained to him it was normal. Between Chance and Eli'el, Kadiri would always be protected.

Chance would listen to music and dance with the kids. They laughed all the time. He would show them his favorite movies. He cut Eli'el's hair, taught him how to box, and even demonstrated how to put cologne on. Before Kadiri could fully walk, she would pull herself up on the furniture and walk from side to side, moving from each piece of furniture until she got to where the action was with her dad and brother.

I observed it all while studying for the online courses I was taking on my computer. My special time with my kids was when I read books to them on the couch. Certain books we read dozens of times, particularly the ones Natelie gave them when I came home from the hospital after having Kadiri. We were finding our rhythm. And just like that, one year had passed, and Kadiri turned one.

16

Failing Love

FALL HAD JUST BEGUN, and it was the week after my birthday. Andrew and I decided to do a barbecue with our immediate family and our two grandmothers in the park. It was a beautiful day. Everyone was happy. Andrew grilled, and we enjoyed a delicious meal. We sat in between decades-old trees in the park, whose leaves were beginning to turn colors. My kids were playing, and Chance and my brothers decided to start a pickup game. Everything seemed fine at first, and then I heard Chance talking under his breath.

Apart

Jonathan was guarding him. Then all of a sudden Chance snapped.

"What up, nigga? You keep fouling me, and you just scratched me!"

Jonathan wasn't backing down. "Man, if I wanted to hit you, I would just hit you!"

Chance's punch hit Jonathan, causing Jonathan to slip on the court. I began screaming, and Andrew rushed over. Jonathan stood up, and he and Andrew both began punching Chance before my dad went ballistic, yelling and shouting,

"Stop it! Everyone, get your things and leave right now! This is not happening!"

I'd never seen my dad so angry in my life. Jonathan had never been in a fight before that moment.

First, I was in shock, then I began to weep uncontrollably.

After I frantically led the kids out of the park, I drove home and called Chance, begging him to come home. He was furious beyond reasoning and began calling his relatives to meet him at the gym. These were family members who were still active in the gang, despite his claims that his gang connections had long been severed.

In a short time, there were a half dozen people at the gym ready to shoot up the house where my grandmother, parents, and brothers lived.

I was terrified and tried to calm myself enough to think without hyperventilating. I continued trying to reason with Chance over the phone, but every time I begged him not to hurt my family, he hung up on me.

My entire family lived with my ninety-one-year-old grandmother, and if he hurt her or anyone else in my family, I would never forgive him. Or myself.

When Chance stopped taking my calls, I called Brother Marquies from church. When I began dating Chance, Brother Marquies warned me of character flaws in him that I wasn't acquainted with yet. But I hadn't listened.

Now I gave him a quick synopsis of what had happened. He asked for Chance's phone number.

About thirty minutes later, Brother Marquies called me back and said he'd talked Chance down. I was relieved, but my heart was broken. I cried for twenty-four hours straight. I went to sleep crying and woke up crying. I cried all night and into the next day. Eli'el cried too.

I never looked at Chance the same after that day.

Any trust I'd had in him was now gone.

He had threatened to kill my family and devastate our children and me.

Never once did Chance apologize. Instead, he took things even further. "My relatives know what your brother's car looks like, and I'm not responsible for what they might do to him."

I resented him more than I loved him, and I was afraid of him too. There was division in our family. I was angry with Jonathan for his comment, and even more angry with Chance for being so immature and starting a fight. I felt so bad for Andrew and for everyone else who had been pulled into a situation they didn't start. How did such a beautiful day turn to one of the worst days of my life? Since becoming an adult, I hadn't been in a disagreement with my brothers. Everyone was angry and hurt.

The next day I went to church and prayed with Sister Dawn. She assured me God already knew that what happened was going to happen, and He already had a solution for the problem. I chose to believe what she said, and about a month and a half later Chance came to church with me. Jonathan was there too and he met us in the vestibule and apologized. After an awkward moment, Chance and Jonathan shook hands.

I hugged Jonathan and said, "Thank you."

Jonathan later told me something that hit me right in the heart: "When Kadiri would look at me, she was afraid. That hurt me deeply, and that day at church God told me to apologize. It was hard yet I did it anyway."

Andrew texted me on New Year's Eve: "I love you." We hadn't spoken in months. I texted back: "I love you, too, Andrew." We were both put in the middle of a situation we never imagined or wanted to be a part of.

Trophy

In the beginning, Chance's attention and time made me feel loved. I'd heard of trophy wives, a notion far below what I ever would've imagined for myself. A trophy represents one's achievement in a particular area. Whereas a crown represents a position one holds until their last breath. A trophy is displayed on a shelf, but a crown is a part of royalty's everyday vesture. A crown is a symbol representing more than an achievement; it exemplifies a person's identity and represents honor, authority, and power. My choices prevented me from walking as myself, a crown; therefore I had become a trophy.

I sat next to my dad on Sunday at the adults' Bible study. He and I always have great conversations, and this day was no different. During the conversation, my dad shared with me a prayer he'd often spoke to God. He said he'd told God I was worthy to be a wife. My eyes watered.

For the first time I began to realize my decision to move in with my fiancé robbed my dad of the opportunity to walk me down the aisle. For my mom to be at my bridal gown fitting, for my children to have the stability of a family, for my best friend to throw me a bridal shower, or for my brothers and family to respect Chance and our relationship.

Instead, in pretending to be his wife, I became the other woman. I was always raised as the one and only; now I was acting like a trophy. Trophies are precarious awards. I have some. The ceremonies where I received each one of them stand out in my mind. Each one represented the work I put in to be recognized for a particular achievement, and I was grateful for being acknowledged.

Growing up, I displayed my trophies in various places because I was proud of them. Over time, though, they were no longer dusted or displayed. Ultimately, they were all put in boxes and moved from the attic to a storage room, then to a shed, and then to the garage. That was the life cycle of my trophies. I've found this is the same for most people with their trophies.

At first, I was precious to Chance. I use the word *precious* because one day as we were leaving my parents' house, my dad looked at Chance and said, "You are getting ready to lose something precious to you if you don't make some changes."

It was a warning to him.

Driving home, Chance got defensive and angry, and his pride emerged. "If your dad has something to say, he should just say it! See, you always have your people in our business!"

"I didn't say anything to my family," I said defensively.

What I didn't tell him was that I never told my family anything bad about our relationship because they wouldn't approve of it if they knew the truth. And even though I hadn't said anything, my family already knew our relationship was awful. Internal dialogues were the norm for me. I never expressed my thoughts or feelings; instead, I shut down. Arguing for days or weeks felt miserable, so silence was my peace. If Chance *really* hurt my feelings, I would eventually speak up and defend myself from his evil imagination.

Through His Eyes

It's destructive when someone else sees and determines your value, and you don't. What happens when they become familiar with you? When they do what it takes to acquire you (the trophy), then, after some time has passed, they decide not to esteem you in the highest regard? What happens when you find out you've been collecting dust and are now being put into a cardboard box and placed into the basement of their heart?

My identity was wrapped up in Chance. Whatever he thought, felt, believed, and said about me was true, and his actions followed. His actions began changing as quickly as leaves in autumn until, ultimately, they fell away. For me, my identity was found in him—a flawed, broken person.

Chance was like me; we were as unstable as the sea. I was so sustained by his attention that I failed to pay attention to me. I didn't compliment myself; I didn't know what was great about me without the gaze of his approval. What about my own gaze? What did I see? I didn't ask myself these questions or find out the answers to them until I left him.

I didn't know I should pay more attention to person's character, lifestyle, and actions more than their words. I didn't ask Chance enough questions. You can never ask too many questions. What he said was he liked me because I was beautiful, I was raised right, I wasn't from the "streets," and I was successful academically and in my career.

He was right: the streets didn't raise me. While I thought he was attracted to my inherent goodness from being raised right, he was actually drawn to me because of how I grew up, which made me naïve. Because I wasn't street smart, I didn't know the colloquialisms and attitudes of the gang culture. I wasn't attracted to men who were a part of the gang lifestyle, yet he assured me he'd lived that life when he was younger and had changed his outlook on life. Unfortunately, the indoctrination of the gang came out when he became angry.

I was so enamored with Chance being attracted to me, and his desire towards me at the time, I didn't notice his attraction to other women. Chance was unfaithful. After a while, when we'd be arguing, I would see his silent phone light up. He claimed he kept it on silent to preserve the battery. His phone would light up with messages from other women saying, "Hey."

Not too incriminating until you consider his overnight stays at the "studio" where his phone didn't have service or was always dead. He'd go to "friend's houses" and couldn't get a ride home, and he didn't want me to pick him up. He would say he was at the gym, but his phone would conveniently die. And when I'd go to pick him up, he wouldn't be where he said he was.

The greatest clue was how much he accused me of cheating and being with other men. When I said goodbye to a male coworker, or said hi to a male classmate at the neighborhood store, he looked on suspiciously, confronting me with accusations.

Behind my back he accused a married brother from my church of being involved with me. I was humiliated time and time again. One time, an old friend I never had a romantic relationship with called me. My brother gave him my phone number because we'd lost touch and he knew our family. Chance accused me of sleeping with him and dozens of other men. Arguments would ensue for days and sometimes weeks at a time.

17

Used-Up Love

THE YEAR 2011 WOULD prove to be one of great transition. Chance was turning thirty. It was the last year of his twenties. I bought him a gift every day of the week to celebrate him. I loved the idea I'd gotten from my coworkers. I thought it was fitting for a thirtieth birthday. We enjoyed our time together. We went to lunch one day and then out to a fancy dinner on the weekend. I felt like the worst days were behind us; maybe we would fall back in love and build a life together after all. We were like a lot of people in their twenties, pursuing relationships, having children, graduating, and pursuing dreams and careers all while trying to find out who we were and our place in the world.

At first, we both tried to fulfill the needs of one another. Temporarily, we were successful in doing this sexually and through companionship. Essentially, we were actors in one another's life script until we could no longer act anymore. Eventually, our true intentions, motives, and needs couldn't be ignored, and we sacrificed our role and our relationship for ourselves, just not all at once.

Throughout the course of our relationship, my value was slowly and steadily diminishing in Chance's eyes. Whenever he had certain business meetings, or particular holiday celebrations on his side of the family, he made sure to let me know so we could attend together. In front of particular people, I was on his arm, and we wore the mask of happiness; otherwise, behind closed doors I was his stepping stool.

Whenever he felt I was excelling or doing well in an area, Chance never celebrated me or allowed me to fully celebrate. His imagination would come up with stories where I was always dishonest, disloyal, and deceitful. He had lost his dream of boxing, and I was slowly and steadily obtaining my dreams. I didn't notice at the time how he'd become jealous and envious of me.

When I began dating Chance, I worked at a bank across town, then I got a job at another bank closer to my home and school. Within the first year of being there, I gave birth to our daughter. He saw firsthand the advancement in my career. I went from being a part-time teller to a full-time teller, then moved from a senior teller to a teller supervisor, then I was promoted to a banker and senior banker before I left the company.

We began dating at the end of my sophomore year in college, and he witnessed the years I went to school full time. He was there when I failed one class and had to retake it. He knew I was tutored, went to study hall, and read about 120 pages a week to keep up with my classes. Not to mention taking notes, studying, completing projects, tests, worksheets, and assignments in between. When I graduated, everyone around me celebrated, except Chance.

My coworkers gave me beautiful gifts: a purse, scarves, jewelry, cards, and a cake. Chance never once said congratulations or even gave me a card or gift. When he saw the gifts, he claimed they were from men at my job, although we were a complete staff of women. Feelings of joy, pride, and gratefulness for my friends and family overwhelmed me. Their genuine love, support, acknowledgement, and generosity blessed me. Fighting to keep those feelings in while experiencing Chance's crushing accusatory words was difficult.

Transitions

I used to have a nightmare that I was with Grandma Murray when she died. I was terrified to be around her in my adolescence from time to time. Years later, Eli'el was in the bedroom with her when she had a stroke, about a month and a half before I graduated from college. We all visited her in the hospital.

I'm grateful I was present when her doctor asked, "How old are you?" and she confidently said, "I'm as old as black pepper."

It seemed like she was going to pull through, then she came down with pneumonia and rapidly declined. The last time I saw her we were alone in her room. I thanked her for everything I could think of as I wept.

"I understand, Grandma. It's okay for you to let go," I said. "I'm going to miss you. You were my constant. I'm going to graduate next week. I know you would have been there if you could have."

Between working, visiting the hospital, caring for my children, finishing my senior year, and arduous arguments with Chance, I found myself in between grieving and celebration. The day before Mother's Day, my grandmother went on to be with Jesus. I found myself choosing an outfit for her funeral and for my graduation; I would be graduating the day after her funeral.

In this she shared her last lessons with me. Sometimes you'll be grieving the last season while being challenged to be present and celebrate the next season. For the last month and a half before graduation, I cried in my car, in the shower, and in the hospital room, grieving my grandmother while simultaneously finishing up my senior projects, taking finals, and studying in each of those moments I had to be present.

On Mother's Day, the sun came up like any other day before. I hated how the day, night, and weeks kept going on, even though I felt like everything should pause because everyone who loved her hadn't moved on. Years later, I learned God gave us the sun to remind us it takes courage to embrace a new day. Although the day is different, somehow, it's still bright. Those who went on before us, provide a love bright enough to reflect throughout the rest of our lives in their absence.

We arrived a few minutes late to my grandma's funeral. They were leading us to the balcony when Chance told the usher, "Nah, this is her granddaughter."

This was one of the only times I was happy he was less agreeable to someone. We ended up a few rows from the podium. Her service was beautiful—the songs, the messages of love, and the sermon. We honored her well. The courage to get up and speak escaped me. I felt overwhelmed, sad, and emotionally drained—numb. As the video of her pictures played in the repast's hall, I found myself wishing she were still there.

After the funeral ended, I dropped Chance off at the gym. Apparently, some investors were coming to the gym that day, so Chance couldn't attend the burial and repasts with me. I said I understood, but the truth was I didn't. I needed him to be there for me. And he wasn't.

Graduation

I woke early the next morning; it was graduation day. It was dreary and lightly sprinkling outside as we got ready, I was concerned about the kids being warm. I was dreading parking and needed to be there on time to get lined up.

Why isn't Chance ready? I told him I had to leave at a certain time!

Chance and I started fighting. I was angry.

"I don't have to be there," Chance said irritatedly. "Don't rush me. Really, you could go on your own!"

I strongly considered his suggestion. I could take my kids with me, park, line up, and have my kids sit with me until some of my family came. Or my kids could walk the stage with me for all I cared. I began crying from frustration and stress. I wanted Chance to be there. I wanted him to be proud of me. He saw how hard I'd worked. I needed him to come be with the kids so I could walk and get my diploma.

His threats ended up being talk, and we finally made it out of the door. As we drove to the campus, I thought, *Will he ever support me? First, it was my grandma's funeral, now this! How is it still about him on my graduation day?*

I rushed to get lined up. It was freezing. I forced myself to not make the day about the drama and to be proud of myself. Walking the stage and receiving my diploma was one of the best feelings I ever had. I knew how much God allowed me to overcome to be there.

In the evening, Aunt Kathy graciously hosted my graduation party. I appreciated her so much. My mom made Mexican food; it was a delicious spread. There were people everywhere. I was so happy to see everyone. They came with smiles, laughs, congratulations, cards, gifts, and hugs. We took tons of pictures. I found myself walking up and down the stairs so I could greet everyone and talk to everyone. I could see Chance getting angrier and angrier.

"Why do you keep going up and down the stairs? What is it? Do you need to be seen?" Chance said angrily.

Even at my graduation party, he was still dictating when we would leave, who I could talk to, and who I was around. I was stunned. *What is he talking about?*

I was talking to all my friends and family throughout the house. It was *my* graduation party, and my grandma's funeral was the day before! Even some people from my dad's side made it.

I appreciated them coming. My elementary school friend, Cherise, was there too. She came with a huge hug, a smile, and a beautiful orchid. Her genuine love and goodness began the first time her family stopped to offer us a ride to school and still exists today.

This is what I was thinking about when I stared back at him in disbelief and told myself not to cry. I didn't have the energy for a scene.

I was hurt by all the emotional strain of the past few months, and it was beginning to catch up with me. I was exhausted. I ate, ignored him, talked with everyone, and allowed myself to be encouraged by the positive words shared with me about my future. The night was still young for my family, but I was drained, so we decided to go home.

Later on in the evening, I sat and read all the cards. I needed those words. I needed to see there were people who genuinely loved and cared for me and were celebrating with me. Chance was supposed to be the one who loved me the most, right? Or at least as much as my parents? Yet as I looked at his behavior, he seemed more foe than friend, more enemy than lover.

18

The End of Our Love

IN JUNE, CELESTE ANNOUNCED she and her boyfriend were going to be married in July. I was excited for her; however, I couldn't help thinking to myself that I was engaged twice as long as she was and still wasn't married. Although their relationship wasn't perfect, I saw they went to counseling and were trying to work on their relationship. I didn't see those qualities in my relationship with Chance.

June

"Cousin, will you be my maid of honor?" Celeste asked. "You've been one of the most consistent people in my life, and you've always been in my corner." I was grateful to stand with her in love and faith on her wedding day.

Celeste's wedding dress shopping landed on the same day as my families June birthday party. It was a beautiful day singing, talking, eating, and watching the kids play at the park. My older cousins and brothers started a pickup game. The time passed quickly, and before I knew it I needed to meet my cousin and aunt at the bridal gown showroom.

"I need to go. Do you mind staying here with my family?" I asked Chance.

"Nah, it's coo," he replied.

Watching my cousin try on gowns was fun. Almost like playing dress-up with a wall full of mirrors. I didn't realize how heavy gowns could be before helping my cousin get dressed. It was three hours later once we found her perfect gown. In between looking at the dresses, I was running after Kadiri and keeping an eye on my cousins' infant son, Richard.

By the time I came back to my family's house to pick up Chance, I was exhausted. Like clockwork, though, he ripped into me as soon as we got in the car, accusing me of being with another man. I looked at him in disbelief.

My thoughts rushed in. *Is he serious? I took our daughter to meet up with another man? Is he crazy? I was with my cousin, my aunt, and our children. He knows that! Why is he ruining a great day?*

Before I could process his accusations, he interrupted my thoughts. "I don't have to be with you. We don't have to be a family. I have other places I could be!"

This became our pattern. On Father's Day, my cousin gave us free tickets to a comedy show. I got dressed up and my parents kept the kids. On the way to dropping them off, we got into yet another an argument.

"Looks like you want to be seen by all these dudes out here," Chance remarked.

I was confused. I was with *him*. My outfit was modest, yet my heart sank, nonetheless. We went to the show and spent the rest of the night arguing. When we returned, he left our apartment. In frustration, I threw a heavy vase at the wall and busted the drywall. Startled, I questioned who I was becoming. I was losing myself.

The saying is true: you see the best and worst in people at funerals and at weddings. It was a beautiful Sunday, and Celeste was getting married. I was running around the house, trying to make sure we were ready to go. Chance was running late again. We began arguing.

"We're going to be late to my wedding!" I yelled, then shook my head and corrected myself. "My cousin's wedding!"

I was irritated with him for not keeping his promises to me and for being so inconsiderate. I took a deep breath. My cousin texted me she was running late. I tried to calm down so I could support her and not get into another argument with Chance. Eventually, we left.

The church service ended, and my family entered into the sanctuary. My dad walked my cousin down the aisle. She looked stunning. Her husband wore the biggest smile. I hadn't witnessed seeing such a big smile on a groom since viewing my parents' wedding photos.

When my cousin cried, I cried too. I knew her getting married was an act of faith, and I was willing to be with her on her faith walk. The best man, Andrew, saw me crying and laid his arm on my shoulder like a brother.

"You all right, sis?" he asked.

I nodded, holding back tears.

We were walking up the isle of the church, and everyone was cheering as pictures were being taken. All our family wore smiles.

I smiled, too, but through my teeth I told Andrew, "I'm fine, but please move your arm. My fiancé is going to lose his mind."

Andrew snatched his arm away. "I didn't mean any harm."

I nodded to him in understanding. I knew he didn't. This was only the second time I'd seen the best man. Once at the rehearsal and now at the wedding. The extent of our communication was a mere introduction; we didn't know one another.

More pictures were taken of the wedding party, and then Chance was mumbling in the background. Some words were coherent, and I began hearing him threatening to fight the best man. Some of my family who heard him frowned.

Humiliation set in again. When my cousin and her husband took their individual shots, Chance stormed up to me with his fist balled.

"So you messin' with this nigga now? You have been actin real funny. It's cool though. I'm gonna get him and you. You can have him!" Chance spat out.

Tears were right behind my eyes. With clinched teeth I said, "What are you even talking about? I don't even know him. He's his friend and he's engaged to be married in a few months! What's your problem? There is nothing I can do about someone else's actions."

In the midst of the chaos, I was called to take more photos. This day wasn't about our dysfunctional relationship. I felt like my entire family was watching me. Once again, our family friend, Brother Marquies, took my fiancé to the side to see if he could reason with him and if he would calm down.

My cousin gave me her bouquet to take to the reception hall, and I got in the car with my kids and Chance. We immediately began yelling and screaming at one another.

"Today, I wanted to be there for my cousin. Instead, you made us late. And now you're accusing me of cheating again. Like you do all the time. And how stupid did you feel when the best man told you he was engaged?"

He didn't apologize or back down.

"I don't care what he said, Marquies said, or you say. Niggas lie every day!" Chance yelled.

I slammed the bouquet down in frustration and immediately regretted it when I saw a few petals fall.

"Drop me off at the gym. I'm not going to the reception."

I felt my heart being crushed. I dropped him off and drove to the reception alone. While I drove, I cried. I'd imagined us dancing together at the reception, another handful of hopes

I'd have to toss onto what was becoming the casket of our relationship.

My brothers sat with my kids and me at the table in silence; this wasn't the place to discuss all my issues. The reception was decorated beautifully. I did my maid of honor speech and meant everything I said. I was happy and hopeful for my cousin, her husband, and their son.

I observed everyone eating, talking, and dancing. One of my cousins was in a fraternity and began dancing like he was on the line. It made me smile.

As the night ended, Brother Marquies came up to me and talked to me about my relationship. "Hey, sis. So, I talked to Chance at the wedding."

I nodded my head I didn't have words.

He leaned back on his right leg, folded his arms, and said, "You know that for a relationship to work, people must change and grow. JayLynn and I are aware that if we mistreat one another and don't make the necessary changes, our relationship won't last. We're both replaceable. She could be with someone else, or I could be if we choose not to change and grow."

I listened and then replied, "Thanks again for your help. The situation could've been a lot worse."

"No problem, sister. I'll be praying for you."

Later that evening, I talked to my mom. This was the second time she saw a glimpse of Chance's anger. She gave me a book and listened to me vent. Then she prayed for me. What stuck out to me the most was at the end of her prayer she said over and over, "It is finished. It is finished. It is finished!"

I told my mom thank you and got off of the phone. I was happy to have the foresight to take the following Monday off. I lay on the couch, my eyes were swollen from crying. The

TV was on, but it was more background noise. Soon after, Chance came in with movies.

"Hey, I got you this movie. I thought you'd like it."

He came in with food from an expensive restaurant we never ate at. *Where'd he get the money?*

As if reading my mind, he said, "I went out with a friend I was working in the studio with."

I mumbled a thank-you for the movie and went to bed.

End Behavior

I loved peace so much I would pretend it existed a lot of the time. Chance was suspicious, cutting, accusatory, and mean. Whenever I did anything he didn't like, like go to a family barbecue he was invited to and didn't want to attend, he'd start an argument. He would do his best to make sure I was upset before I went. He'd leave while I was at the family function with the kids and wouldn't say where he was going. He wouldn't talk to me for days or sometimes weeks.

"You weren't with you family!" he'd say, or some other outlandish accusation like, "You met up with some other man you've been talking to."

I'd always look at him in amazement and say, "With our kids?"

Every time this would happen, my feelings were so hurt. I cried not because his accusations were true but because he didn't know me. Deeper than the realization of not being known was the fact he didn't trust me. How did I have a child with someone who didn't know me or trust me after all the years we spent together?

To compound the dysfunction, whenever I would support or help someone who wasn't him, he would start arguing with me. One such instance was when I paid for some beverages to help contribute to my cousin's wedding. He got upset and said, "You don't support me."

On several occasions I paid for his studio sessions and various other things, including all our living expenses.

Another time one of my brothers was in a bad place, and we were concerned about him. As a family, we talked and prayed together for hours. Chance began calling me nonstop. I was afraid and thought there may be an emergency. I answered the phone, panicked, once I saw the missed calls.

"Hey, I just saw you called. Is everything okay? What's wrong?"

He never answered me, he just asked, "What are you doing?"

"I'm just talking and praying with my family," I said. "We're at my grandma's house. So what's going on?"

He cut me off. "Never mind. You're just with your people. You're never there for me." Then he hung up.

Chance never told me what was going on with him that night. He never checked in to see if my brother or my family were okay. Learning about emotional abuse causes me to question if anything was ever wrong at all.

My belief was if I constantly accepted his behavior, he would see I accepted him unconditionally. This was all in hopes he would in turn accept me fully. Acceptance never came.

Part 5

Finding Love

19

Kindergarten Love

WITH PAPERWORK IN HAND, I took Eli'el and Kadiri to check out three kindergarten programs. I was excited. Eli'el was so bright, and he loved to learn. As we left the last school and got into the car, Eli'el began talking. He didn't talk to me about our cousin's beautiful wedding and reception the day before; instead, he began repeating what he had heard Chance and I saying to each other.

He recited the argument word for word, almost like he was asking if he'd understood the situation right. He grasped what I was attempting to communicate. While sitting in the parking lot in front of the school, I turned my head and looked in my back seat. Both my children stared back at me. I looked from Eli'el to Kadiri and back again.

In that moment, I realized Chance and I were teaching Eli'el and Kadiri through our arguments. I was teaching my son it was okay to speak to and treat a woman like Chance treated me. Although our daughter wasn't even two yet, soon enough I would begin teaching her it was okay to be spoken to and treated like her father spoke to and treated me. Over the next several weeks, I reflected. Changes needed to be made soon. We weren't being a good example to our children.

Being a parent was serious to me. My little people, an endearing phrase I used to describe my kids, were dependent on us to show them the way. I didn't want to mess up my kids' mentalities and, ultimately, their lives by my inability to get along with Chance. I wanted our relationship to work; however, we'd both need to change.

I began looking up articles at work about abuse. As I was reading, I could see our behavior in the pages. I printed off an article about verbal and emotional abuse and I wondered, *How will I approach him about this? How should I ask him to go to counseling with me?*

Night

The next couple of weeks were quieter than usual. We didn't talk often, and our intimacy was diminishing. I felt like a zombie. I wasn't distracted with school. Usually, we did better when I wasn't in school. Not this time; this time was different.

I'm not sure how the argument started. Chance began accusing me of being with the best man and threatened to hurt us.

"I'm going to find out," he assured me. "I'm coming for you and that nigga on Bloods!"

"Good!" I yelled back. "It will be a relief once you find out nothing happened!"

I tried to leave to the grocery store to get our daughter some medicine. He slammed the front door and locked it.

"Chance, just let me go to the store," I pleaded. He began yelling and threatening me even more. Terror filled me.

What if he hits me? A few times he's already grabbed me where I couldn't move and pushed me. I ran to the bathroom in our room and tried to slam the door. It hit his forearm. I looked up in terror to see he'd moved his arm, then I closed the door and locked it.

"You hit my arm!" he yelled through the door.

"Please just go away," I cried.

I sat on the floor of our bathroom and prayed as tears rolled down my cheeks.

I recited a scripture I'd just memorized from Hebrews 13:6. "The LORD is my helper; I will not fear. What man can do to me?" Eventually, Chance stopped yelling. It was getting late. I had an early shift and needed to go to sleep.

I came out of the bathroom timidly. He was sitting on the couch.

The first thing he said was, "Oh, and I would be wrong if I hit you, right? After you slammed my arm in the door?"

"You threatened me," I quietly reminded him. Then I added, "I didn't mean to hit your arm."

He gave me a side eye. Tears flowed down my face with reckless abandon. He looked at me and huffed out a sigh.

Exasperated, he said, "Man, stop crying. I hate when you cry. You cry all the time."

I wiped my tears and changed for bed, then I cried silently in bed. He laid down beside me and held me tighter than he ever had. I was terrified.

What if he chokes me? What if he hits me with something in our room? I began thinking of what I needed to do next. *What am I going to do? Where am I going to go? Will he let me leave for work tomorrow morning?*

I looked over at the clock; it was past 4:00 a.m. I was exhausted but didn't dare go to sleep. I began bracing myself for the day. All I knew was that this couldn't happen again. I might die the next time, and our children would be left motherless. I needed a plan.

My alarm clock went off. I got up and showered and got ready for the day. I drove to work and wondered how I even got there. I tried to put my best foot forward and help each client who stood in front of me. On my lunch break I talked to

Chance. It was worse than small talk. I didn't have words, and it didn't seem he did either. I needed to stop avoiding what needed to be said.

I took a deep breath and said, "What happened last night was unacceptable. You scared me. I want to work on our relationship. In the meantime, though, we need boundaries."

"Boundaries? Nigga, we don't need boundaries!" Chance shouted through the phone.

The realization that he saw nothing wrong with what happened between us the night before was disturbing. I began weeping uncontrollably. We did need boundaries.

What I'd accepted was unacceptable. Chance threw accusations at me constantly. Our relationship had become a secret competition shrouded in pretend support. He purposely didn't compliment, congratulate, or celebrate any of my successes. His jealously was directed towards any relationship I had that wasn't with him. He promised to marry me, to help with provision, to work together for "our family," yet in the end he threatened to kill my family and me.

Every promise he made he always broke, and he never took accountability to change or grow. He consistently said and did hurtful things, then he'd demean me by calling me a crybaby. Who knows how many times he cheated on me and lied while taking advantage of my loyalty towards him?

All the while he devalued our relationship, which caused me to live in a state of fear and uncertainty. Staying in our relationship validated Chance's unacceptable behavior. I was never expecting Chance to be perfect, yet it was his lack of empathy, maturity, and personal transformation that continually wounded all of us. This was about me not normalizing abuse.

I got off the phone with Chance, called the manager of our apartment, and asked for a copy of our lease. I began looking up what the non-emergency 911 number was. *Could I get a police escort?*

It was time to move. One manager at my branch asked if I was okay, and I told her as little as I could. My shift was over, and Chance picked me up. As we drove I thought, *We're not safe. How can I get out of this lease?*

I dropped him off at the gym and headed to our apartment to get the leasing agreement. As I drove, I confided in an older woman, Jenny, who assured me I was doing the right thing. She shared her experiences. They paralleled mine with such precision it was eerie.

I loved and respected Jenny, yet I didn't want to be going through these same situations in my forties and fifties. A few weeks earlier, I openly shared with Celeste that Chance had grabbed me and pushed my head in a recent argument.

Calmly, Celeste said, "That's how it all starts. If you don't leave your relationship now, you'll be like Jenny twenty-five years from now."

I knew she was right.

Confrontations

After I got a copy of our lease agreement, I read through all of it. There was no way out. I took it with me and went to my grandma's house. Finally, I told my family the truth, something I hadn't done in a long time.

"I don't feel safe with me and the kids living in my apartment with Chance anymore."

That's all my brothers and dad needed to hear.

"Where's he at?" Andrew asked.

I didn't respond, afraid the confrontation would start another fight, or worse. My brothers and dad used deductive reasoning and drove up to the gym and confronted him.

Andrew asked him if what I told them was true. Chance confirmed what I said was true. To which Andrew replied, "Stephanie's not with you anymore. Our family will no longer be threatened, mistreated, or disrespected by you. This is over. She and the kids are moving out today."

I was on my way to our apartment and wasn't present for the conversation. But I knew when it ended because my phone began to ring nonstop. As soon as I heard Chance's ringtone and saw his name light up my screen, I began shaking.

I was on the phone with Celeste, trying to figure out what I should do next. I frantically said, "He's calling me! Chance is calling me again."

"Okay, you don't have to answer," she stated calmly.

I felt peace. *That's right*, I thought to myself. *I don't have to answer. Why didn't I know that?*

Moving Out

My kids stayed with my mom, and Celeste assured me she would watch Kadiri for me in the morning so I could go to work. My aim was to move all of my things out of the apartment besides the furniture. It was painful being there. Every room held a memory of an argument, tears, shoves, and threats.

Packing became feverish.

What if he shows up?

My dad and brothers arrived and began loading boxes into my truck and Andrew's car. I cried the entire time, ignoring at least forty phone calls and text messages from Chance.

My dad looked at me as if he already knew my thoughts, "It's never a waste to love someone."

I looked back at him numbly.

Was this the end? If in the end there was no happily ever after like in the fairy-tale stories I read as a child. So now what? We went through all the pain for nothing? All those conversations, arguments, altercations, suspicions, lies, and deceit broke down the castle of our lives from the inside. It was treason. It took so much effort to wave the white flag of defeat, to leave the castle and just fall.

No one wants to say they endured, prayed, forgave, talked, and confided, only to find that in the end it was all for nothing! There was no relationship or family to hold on to. Our brokenness had defeated us, and the reward was cold and empty.

It was two o'clock in the morning when we finished taking the last of the boxes into my grandma's second house where Jonathan was staying. He made space for my children and me to stay there too. My phone began to ring again. I didn't need to look at who was calling me, but I answered. He sounded different than I'd ever heard him. He sounded concerned, yet he confronted me right away.

"Aye, yo! So your brothers and your pops came up here. Are you serious? He came up here and asked me about yesterday."

Immediately, I went into defense mode. "I didn't tell them where you were. They just went up there I asked them not to—"

He cut me off. "Your bro was respectful when they came up here to the gym."

I let out a sigh of relief.

"You got my pops all upset with me like I'm really an abuser. Is what your brother said true? You don't want to be with me?"

"I didn't say that" I replied hurriedly.

He began talking fast almost to himself. "See, they don't want you to be with me."

This was the first time he'd ever let on he cared what my family thought about him.

"This is crazy! Why'd you do this? I just got home and almost everything is gone. It doesn't feel right here without you and the kids."

I cried silently. I didn't say anything new. I said the same things I'd been saying for years. "At the end of the day, we did the relationship exactly how you wanted to do it. It's not working. Not only is it not working, it is getting worse. We need counseling. We need help to heal and move forward in our relationship. And we both need to change."

As the weeks passed, Chance and I talked more. The plan was that our children and I would stay with my family. I'd pay for our apartment for the next four months, and he could stay until the lease was up. I would bring the kids to him so he could watch them while I went to work, and we would work to mend our relationship. We tried to communicate; it was strained at best.

One Saturday I asked, "What are you doing today?"

"Hopefully, doing you," he replied.

I considered his proposition before turning him down. "I love you, but I'm not ready." I shuttered thinking that the last time I was in his arms I was suffocating.

"Just come back home, Stephanie. This is crazy."

When I tried to explain why that didn't make sense, he abruptly cut me off. "You just want to be with your family. You're where you want to be!" He hung up.

Slowly, he began not answering my calls, or his phone would be dead. Or when I asked him what he was up to, he would say ambiguous things. I began to not trust him even more. He couldn't even commit to being there for the kids while I worked.

It was a hard, confusing time. With every interaction nothing changed. He began demeaning me and making me feel guilty because I had left, and he claimed to have nowhere to go.

I tried to reason with him. *He had the apartment! What is he talking about?*

Days later, I went to the apartment to do some cleaning. The house hadn't been opened in over a week. I could tell. It was stuffy, and a week's worth of dishes remained in the sink.

He was lying. He was staying somewhere, but it wasn't here. No wonder he wouldn't say I could drop the kids off with him when I went to work.

We planned to talk the next day to begin figuring out our new schedule. He didn't answer his phone. I began panicking, trying to figure out how to get to work on time and who could care for our children. Celeste said she could continue to help me. So I began the trek out to her house, then to my job, then back to her house, then back home five days a week.

Driving in the car over two hours a day was normal. On my commute I listened to worship CDs while yelling at people in traffic. Kadiri began mimicking me. Most of the time she was singing worship songs, but sometimes I heard her yelling for people to "Goooooooo!" from the back seat. I liked it. I was proud and embarrassed at the same time.

Calling It

One day I was driving Chance to the apartment. I had asked a few people to pray for me. I needed to end my relationship and engagement, and once again he began threatening my family and me.

One night I got the courage to ask, "Would you actually shoot up my grandmother's house with my entire family, including our daughter?"

He shrugged. "I can't control what my relatives do."

I was anxious and fearful. I had told Celeste about his threats, and she got angry and spoke Scripture to me. "Touch not my anointed and do my prophets no harm! God will protect you. Chance can't do nothin'!"

I wanted to be strong like her, and I wanted to believe too. Tears rolled down my cheeks. Over the last few years it felt as if tears etched out a pathway down my face. I was tired of crying. I didn't want my kids to grow up with a mom who was afraid, sad, and crying all the time.

I spoke and my voice quivered. "I can't be with you anymore."

His accusations fell on deaf ears as we sat in the car.

It was one of the saddest days of my life seeing him get out of the car, walk down the dark steps, and disappear behind the door into our apartment. I saw his shoulders heave. I'd only seen him cry one time before when his grandmother died. He was hurt and angry.

I began weeping as I backed out of the parking lot and made my way home. I gave it my all. I had tried so hard. We both had tried at different times, but it's like we could never work hard together. I was exhausted of it all. Even if he wouldn't admit it, this was what was best.

20

The Love of a Community

IN THE MONTHS LEADING up to our breakup two significant instances happened. At work I received a bonus and decided to buy some worship CD's. My soul felt dark, and I was getting tired of the music I was listening to. Consciously, I waited until 8 a.m. to call Jonathan.

"Hello." Jonathan said when he answered the phone.

"Hey Jonathan, I just wanted to tell you. I feel like I'm coming out of some darkness. I don't exactly know what that means. I just wanted to tell you that. Okay have a good day."

"Okay you too."

"I love you."

"I love you too, bye."

One night I had a vivid dream Chance was tearing me down with his words and we were standing on either side of our bed arguing. In the dream I interrupted him and began saying loudly, "Actually I'm this and actually I'm that..." Then I woke up.

As I sat in the darkness, I meditated on my Grandma Murray's words.

She'd say, "All you have is your name and your word."

I was giving away both.

After we broke up, people began sharing their observations. People considered me educated, talented, attractive, and kind and were puzzled as to why I had been attracted to Chance in the first place. Through conversations with Chance, people recognized his selfishness, anger, pride, and ambitious nature along with his lack of concern for our family. The one thing I cared the most about was not his priority, and it showed through in simple conversation. I berated myself, wondering why I had been so blind.

Close Calls

A few weeks after our breakup, I was at Matthew's high school football game. It was cold and dark, yet bright on the field. Matthew and his teammates were having a phenomenal game. We were standing and cheering when my phone rang. I looked down; it was an unknown number. I answered.

As I answered the phone the crowd roared, so I could barely hear the woman on the other end. "Hello? Hello? Is this Stephanie Murray? Can you hear me?"

"Hi! Yes, I can hear you," I assured.

She continued, giving me her name. "I'm a pharmacist at King Soopers, and I'm calling to inform you that your birth control has been recalled. You can come into the store to get a free refill."

I looked at my phone and then back at the field. Everything went blurry. I heard what she'd said, I just couldn't believe it. *What were the chances? What if I had slept with Chance last week?*

Knowledge and Instruction

Life changed drastically. The term "sublease" entered into my consciousness, but I don't recall how. I investigated what a sublease was and then prayed. Our apartment was full of furniture, and Chance wasn't staying there, so I decided to sublease our apartment. I called Chance and talked to him about it. I wasn't emotional. I was matter-of-fact. I'd paid for our entire household for close to three years by myself when he was supposed to have helped. I asked him if he'd break the lease with me and give up our deposit so we could sublease it. He agreed. I could barely believe my ears.

When we were together, we planned to buy a house the following year. I still wanted to buy a house even if it was by myself. I began taking first-time homebuyer classes, and the time was passing quickly. If I could save the money from the apartment, I would be in a better situation financially to buy my first home. I was relieved.

I contacted our apartment building, and they gave me the go-ahead. I posted my furniture and apartment on Craigslist. My family and I cleaned the apartment from top to bottom, including the carpets, and it looked great. I met up with a couple of people who weren't truly interested.

As I was praying one day, I felt God speaking to my heart to rewrite the ad and republish it, so I did. Within a day a young man and his brother subleased our apartment without even seeing it. They went to the office, applied, and did the background checks. I went to the apartment a few more times to move the furniture out.

Celeste and her husband purchased everything, so I didn't have to store it. As I was finishing everything up, Chance began texting me.

"I thought you were moving. I saw your car."

I looked up, startled. *He doesn't have a car. How does he know I was there? Is he following me?*

I hurriedly shot a text back: "I'm getting the last of my things. Someone took over the lease."

A different week my wisdom teeth were extracted, and I was resting at my grandmother's home. I got three missed calls in a row. I thought something had happened. It was Chance.

"Why is your car at your grandma's house? Why aren't you at work?"

I felt uneasy and obliged to tell him my situation. "I had my wisdom teeth taken out." I didn't want to see him. I was afraid, so I remained still on the couch.

Even though we were broken up, I felt like I was still accountable to him. We began arguing a lot every time he'd call or text. I wondered to myself when this was all going to end.

One day we were in a heated argument, and I yelled, "It doesn't matter anymore! It doesn't matter anymore!"

We hung up. An hour or so later he texted: "I can't believe you said it doesn't matter anymore."

But it doesn't.

I needed to let myself know as much as I needed to let him know that all the things we used to argue, fuss, and fight over no longer mattered because we weren't together. He would pop up as the holidays came to ask how we were and say he missed us. The things he would say infuriated me.

Why did he say he missed us when he constantly said he didn't have to be there when we were together? I vented my frustrations to my friends and family, and their truth hurt as much as it helped me. One time Chance claimed he missed me and Andrew stated, "He misses you paying his rent." I laughed so hard I almost cried. One of the most shocking parts of healing is when you find your laugh regardless of the pain.

Another shocking part of healing is how simple instructions push you ahead. I began hating how my ex still had emotional and psychological control over me even though we weren't together. I spoke to a woman from my church, Sister

Jay. She witnessed me growing up, falling away, and coming back to God. In the process, she became an older sister to me.

As we stood in the foyer at church a man asked, "Where's your man at?"

"I don't have a man!" I exclaimed.

He was shocked and hurriedly said, "I'm sorry to hear that."

"I'm proud of you!" Sister Jay said. "I was wondering how you were going to handle that question."

I opened up to her about the fear, anxiety and daily arguments I was still having with Chance.

She looked at me and said, "Just scroll through his text messages, and if you don't see your daughter's name, delete the message and don't respond."

I considered what she said, and she was right. When I read the messages, I would argue with him about his warped recollection of our relationship woes. I didn't need to defend myself or argue. All we needed to do was work together to raise our daughter. Kadiri was now our only connection. Within the week I heard the Pastor Ron Carpenter say, "Whatever you speak to lives, and whatever you ignore dies."

Even though we were no longer together, my emotions were still being controlled by his actions. This was how was he still controlling me from afar. I chose to listen to Sister Jay and delete the messages. The first few times, I was tempted to read the messages and just not respond. I quickly realized I needed to listen to exactly what she said. Anything he said would always be the same thing he'd said before.

Nothing changed, and I needed to stop breaking my own heart by reading the messages in hopes he'd changed. He hadn't. He'd rejected changing with me, so I would have to go on my transformative journey without him. It's not what I wanted, yet it was reality, and I needed to tell myself the truth.

After all, what Andrew said was right: "Self-deception is the worst kind of deception."

I deleted countless messages without reading them and began to have more peace and less anxiety.

In Their Pain

I was regaining my joy even though it was hard raising two kids by myself. My son asked me about us moving out and me breaking up with Chance. I tried to answer him in age-appropriate honesty. We cried as we held hands in the car.

"So Chance doesn't want to be my dad anymore?" Eli'el asked.

"No, it's not that," I explained. "We are just not together anymore, and you still have your dad."

He shook his head angrily. "It isn't the same seeing my dad on the weekends and living with him."

We both cried harder.

My son began preschool in the fall and then began expressing his hurt through anger. There were parent teacher conferences, emails, and phone calls, as well as suspensions. This lasted the next three years. It was difficult navigating my own pain and Eli'el's pain at the same time.

However, with God's grace He sent caring teachers who partnered with me to encourage my son so he could get better. One teacher realized he wasn't a bad child; he was angry and needed help with his emotions. Eli'el began going to classes to learn about and manage his emotions. Slowly, he got better. We both did.

Back to School

My mindset, attitude, and beliefs had been severely shaken and put through the fire. Everything had disintegrated, besides my hope to know and understand what love really was. What was it I kept saying I wanted and yet it always seemed to elude me? Why was it I failed in so many relationships? What did my parents do so their love remained over the years? I began to study the Bible beyond the words. I sought to understand it.

"When the student is ready the teacher appears," is a common saying. Hearing the years of unanswered questions answered became the norm. Questions I never even uttered. Questions I didn't allow myself to think about by making myself busy raising my kids, working, and going to school. I had suppressed them and pushed them down long enough, and now they required answers. I wasn't going to be able to ignore them any longer.

Almost daily I was confronted with a lie I believed and walked in for many years through the teaching and preaching CDs I consumed during my commute. Jonathan introduced me to Ron Carpenter's ministry, and I finally felt like someone knew what my struggles were and how to help me overcome them. He said the things that needed to be said. The lessons were raw, truthful, biblical, and transparent. I didn't have to hide. His ministry already knew about my sort of brokenness. I heard phenomenal preaching all my life; however, I began to realize certain beliefs and practices I was taught prevented me from transformation.

I was unsure of what the future held, yet I knew I needed to possess courage to take my masks off. It was time to stop hiding and playing the pretty and put-together woman. I needed to know what the Bible said about my personal struggles and what I could do to overcome them before they destroyed me.

The end of myself had come. Like Carpenter said, "Some people's pain tolerance is too high." My pain tolerance had run out.

I was willing to try the principles in the Bible to see if I could personally experience what others described as the life-changing transformational power of God. I was grateful to be with my children in what Jonathan described as a place safe enough to cultivate healing, change, growth, and transformation.

I began to go to church with expectation instead of obligation for the first time in many years. It seemed like the pastors were always confirming something I'd felt God speaking to my heart in my personal or corporate times of prayer. Even topics I had begun studying would be mentioned in their sermons. One day I felt God speaking to my heart I was like a toddler. As I looked at Kadiri, I began seeing myself.

Kadiri was beginning to walk, feed herself, and get dressed on her own. She was learning how to speak, listen, play, and she was curious. Her changes were so drastic from month to month, and she was becoming a more mature version of her previous self. I was beginning to feed my soul with the Bible, sermons, and Christian music. I was reading books, praying, and studying to do the right thing instead of pretending like I believed the truth. Pretense had led my life down a path of destruction.

21

Sacrificial Love

EVERYONE AROUND ME SEEMED to be going through life-altering transitions. To find some stability, I often went to our family friend's home. I refer to them as my big brother and sister, Brother Marquies and Sister Jay. They allowed my family and me to listen to a teaching series from John Bevere called "Breaking Intimidation." I took pages and pages of notes. When the series ended, we prayed and worshipped together. When we left, I knew I was fundamentally different.

Afterward, going through this teaching I could feel and sense when someone attempted to intimidate me. At work there was a disgruntled, disrespectful customer who established an ugly reputation. I was waiting on him, and he began to try to rush me as I was counting his deposit. I was getting flustered and could feel my heart begin to race and my hands started shaking. I was filled with fear until I realized I was the one who was making the deposit, and if I made a mistake, I would get written up, not him. He needed me.

So I choose not to be affected by his bad attitude and demands. I was going to slow down and make sure I didn't make any mistakes. It turned out I made a mistake, and me slowing down helped me catch it. His grumbling, rude demeanor, and harshness wouldn't control my behavior.

Intimidation had tripped me up for a long time, but gratefulness now filled my heart because I could recognize it.

Another moment changed the trajectory of my life during one of my commutes. I was sitting in my car listening to a sermon when I began weeping so profusely, I had to pull over to the side of the road. Ron Carpenter was teaching about oxen and yokes. An ox is a castrated bull used as a draft animal. In his sermon he stated oxen are extremely strong and virtually untamable animals within their natural state.

However, for farmers to use oxen to plow their fields they must first domesticate them, and they start when they are young. When oxen are young, a yoke is put on their necks, and as they grow bigger larger yokes are placed on them. A yoke is a wooden crosspiece fastened over the necks of two animals and attached to the plow or cart they pull together.

The oxen comply to the farmer's enforced demands because they are unaware; they are stronger than the yoke. They are unaware they are stronger than the yoke because they have been restrained by a yoke from their youth. Carpenter went on to say people are ensnared with various vices in their youth. Yokes are placed on us on purpose to keep us bound the rest of our lives.

As I listened it occurred to me: I had been molested. Before that moment at twenty-five years old, I never acknowledged my own violation. I only acknowledged violating others. My molestation was different than the infractions I'd heard from other people, which is why I'd never identified it as molestation. Molestation was the yoke of my youth. I cried out to Jesus to set me free of the hurt, shame, and self-hatred I'd carried for over twenty years because of what was done to me and what I subsequently did. I didn't want to be yoked anymore. Suddenly, I felt the grace, love, and mercy of the

Lord fill my car. These grace-filled moments continued my healing process.

Through further teaching from Carpenter, I began to learn how important it was to look at the patterns in my life. If I didn't acknowledge the patterns and subsequent lies I believed, there was no chance of me changing the direction of my life. I began journaling and wrote down a list of things I personally did that caused my life to be one I didn't like living. I wrote down the characteristics of the men I kept attracting. I fasted for a week. Each day I focused on sins I wanted to overcome.

At the end of the week, I prayed with my mom, Celeste, Sister Dawn, and Sister Jay. As we prayed, Sister Jay shared some insights she'd received from God. "The root of the sins in your life is low self-esteem."

When I heard what she said, I thought it seemed so simple, yet those were never words I would have used to describe myself. I was consumed in what I considered more alarming words like control, bitterness, fear, abuse, and lust.

All the while, my low self-esteem created the intricate root system and established the tree of bad fruit in my life. This was a defining moment in my transformation. After the prayer meeting, I was delivered from low self-esteem. I began to see myself as God saw me, and because of my renewed heart and mind, my behavior changed to.

A few months later our pastor challenged the church to read the entire Bible in forty days and to fast sometime during the forty days. We were headed into the holiday season and into the New Year. Jonathan and I were talking about reading the Bible and fasting. He mentioned he was going to fast, so I asked him what kind of fast he was going to do and for how long. I expected him to say a three-day fast, or maybe a seven-day fast. At most, a twenty-one-day Daniel's fast. What I heard him say I never could've fathomed.

"I'm going to fast for forty days," Jonathan declared.

Immediately, I heard the voice of Lord speak to my heart. *And so are you, Stephanie.*

I looked at him, dumbfounded, and asked follow-up questions. "Oh, are you going to do the Daniel's fast the first twenty-one days?"

"No, I'm just going to drink juice and water for forty days," Jonathan said.

Immediately, I replied, "I feel like I'm supposed to do it with you, but I think I will do the Daniel's fast first."

As soon as I made the statement, I heard the Lord speak to my heart again. *You will do it exactly like Jonathan is doing it.*

I looked at my brother, bewildered, and told him what I heard. Jonathan got excited, yet I was unsure. We bought a book together by Jentezen Franklin called *Fasting* and read it cover to cover before we began.

One of the most impactful parts of the book was when he spoke about the life cycle of flies. He said when farmers are trying to exterminate flies who are killing their crops, they must spray for forty days straight, and if they skip the fortieth day, the second generation of flies will live and the process will begin again. He wrote about how the devil is called the lord of the flies and how there are problems and troubles in our lives that have lived on generationally. But through fasting and prayer, God can help end these curses in our bloodlines. So, Jonathan and I began.

I wrote down a list of forty people and situations I wanted to focus on during my fast. Every day I focused on the reasons why I wanted to make it through the fast. I began to notice everyday whatever my reason or focus was, there was a message or situation showing me I was on the right path, which kept me from ending our fast prematurely.

We quickly began to notice that when we read the Bible, we physically felt fuller. I was most clear and at peace when I was at home reading the Bible, and at times when I was at church. I did my best to journal and write down everything I was learning and studying. Only by the instruction and grace of God did we complete it.

Confessing Faults

Jonathan and I finished fasting. The topic of abortion came up multiple times in a two-week period. Every time I heard the word, I felt sick and became filled with sorrow. I kept feeling like I needed to tell Jonathan about my abortion, and I didn't want to. I knew this information would hurt him and my family.

I tried my best to get out of confessing this fault. I told the Lord, "It's not like it's a secret. I told my two best friends."

God reminded me of the scripture in James 5:16: "Confess your faults one to another, and pray one for another, that ye may be healed" (KJV). My friends and I hadn't prayed together.

I felt God speaking to my heart to be transparent. I looked up the word in order to convince myself I already was transparent and didn't need to disclose to Jonathan about my abortion. My plan was to just beg God again, again, and again if He would please forgive me. Transparent means "free from pretense or deceit" and "easily seen through." That's when I knew it was time to share with my brother the worst thing I'd ever done.

I was nervous and ashamed. Jonathan and I sat on a bench on the porch of our grandmother's house and looked into the evening sky. I didn't know how to start. So I started with the truth.

"Jonathan, it's hard for me to hear about abortions because I had an abortion between my conception of Eli'el and Kadiri." I paused. "Having an abortion is the worst thing I've ever done. I was overcome with so much fear. I didn't believe I could survive raising another child by myself, and most of all I didn't want to."

I looked down before continuing. "I regret my decision, and I have genuine remorse. Even though the circumstances hadn't changed when I got pregnant with Kadiri, despite being on birth control, I choose to be a mother again and to trust God, even if I ended up alone. Anyway, God's been dealing with my heart about transparency, and I felt I needed to share this with you. I'm very sorry. I don't think I will ever be able to forgive myself."

Jonathan sat there, shocked, but he was also gracious. Suddenly, he stood up and told me to stand up too. At six three, he stood in front of my five-two frame with his back to me, then he reached his arm out behind him to cover me.

"God, cover Stephanie from the tormenting spirits of shame, condemnation, fear, and self-hatred that consistently attack her because of her sin," he prayed. "I ask that all these spirits will no longer have access to her soul, for neither is she the city nor is she the gate."

My choice to have an abortion had opened the city of my life and the gate of my soul to more pain than I could bear. Shedding innocent blood, murder, hate, guilt, shame, fear, sorrow, depression, and condemnation had plagued my mind. My brother's grace toward me made James 5:16–17 my own personal testimony: "Confess your faults one to another, and pray for one another, that ye may be healed. The effectual fervent prayer of a righteous man availeth much" (KJV). After my confession and Jonathan's prayer over me, I felt forgiven and redeemed for the first time.

Yes, I'm still sad at times. I will never know who my second child was. It pains me greatly, especially when I see how wonderful my other children are every day. They teach me more about Jesus and more about myself as I see them grow, and especially when they make me laugh.

The other day thoughts I'd never allowed myself to think overwhelmed me. I wanted to apologize to my baby. *Will I ever have the opportunity to say I'm sorry I didn't love you because I didn't love myself? Is my baby in heaven with Jesus?*

Jesus promised people that if their mother or their father forsook them, that He would take them up (Psalm 27:10). I didn't have any answers to any of my questions, so I prayed, "Lord Jesus, can my baby and all the other babies forever be in Your arms? I don't believe I have the right to ask, yet if You could answer me I'd appreciate it. And even if You don't, I know You know what's best for me. I trust You."

Within moments, Sister Jay texted me she wanted to share a song with me, and she hoped I had a blessed day. The song she shared was "You Still Love Me" by Koryn Hawthorne. The lyrics spoke directly to my heart, right after the words of my heart left my lips and he heard me and responded, he still loved me in spite of my mistakes.

Home

While living with my grandmother, I was in the process of working with Jacque´, my Realtor, to find a home of our own. One night I had a dream of a home with white tile floors. I told Jacque´ about my dream and asked, "Have you seen any homes with white tile floors?"

"No I haven't seen any homes with white tile. If I do, I'll let you know right away!"

We spent months looking at small and big homes, strange layouts, fixer-uppers, and nice homes whose HOA fees were too hefty. We walked into some homes and walked right back out. It was quite a process.

Then one day I got an email from Jacque´ with "Stephanie's Home" in the subject line. I looked at the pictures and became ecstatic. The light tile in the kitchen reminded me of my dream. We went to go see it and put in an offer the same day.

While we were waiting to close on the house, my grand-mother's house was in such need of repair that I felt my children and I were no longer in a suitable space. I called one of my friends from church, Sister Dawn, and asked if we could stay with her until I closed on my home.

Sister Dawn and her sons, Jennis and Jair, hosted us graciously. They loved us and allowed us to share their space. My children were finally sleeping on beds and not on the couch. We enjoyed laughs, love, and genuine day-to-day kindness. Sister Dawn and I talked and prayed together, and I learned so much from her.

In the meantime, the process of closing on our house was not going smoothly. Intimidation, lies, changing the selling price on paperwork, and resistance for every reasonable thing we asked for turned the experience into one long trial. At one point, Jacque´ said my deal was in the top five most difficult deals she'd done in twenty years of being in the business.

I was stressed out. Yet after every negative interaction, I was reassured by Jacque´, yet the opposition was unrelenting.

After one particular grueling day, Sister Dawn asked, "What's going on?"

I shared with her the latest episode in the soap opera.

She simply looked at me and asked, "Do you trust God?"

Tearfully, I said, "I'm trying my best to."

We prayed together. That evening as I did laundry, I listened to "All Things Are Working" by Fred Hammond on repeat.

One month later, final papers were signed, and my children and I moved into a place of our own.

It was, literally, the house of my dreams.

Once again, God showed me that I could trust Him. He had never failed me, and He never would.

22

The Restoration of Love

DURING THIS TRANSITION, I began to attend Pure Apostolic Works, a church that encouraged the congregants to study and teach lessons on our struggles. We would share our lessons on Wednesdays. It's called Developmental Wednesdays. I grew more in a year than in decades going to church through participating in this practice.

One year, I was teaching a short series on envy. I wanted to make the point that people have struggles we aren't privy to, and that we should always be kind and loving toward one another. As I prepared the lesson, I jotted down some of the difficult times in my life, including being molested through a game called "house," and then going on to teach other children the same "game."

I had never shared this story publicly. In fact, my own parents didn't know what had happened to me. On the Wednesday I was supposed to teach the lesson, I began to have doubts. I pulled Sister Jay aside.

"There's a story in the first part of my testimony, and I don't know if I should share it. Can you pray with me to see if I am supposed to share it?" I asked quietly.

We prayed together.

Then, without knowing the story I was unsure about telling, she heard from the Lord and said, "Indeed, you will."

Except she didn't say it once.

She said it three times: "Indeed, you will. Indeed, you will. Indeed, you will."

I swallowed hard. After the opening worship, I got up to teach and felt the Spirit of God all around me as I shared the lesson.

When the lesson was over, Sister Jay walked up to me with tears in her eyes. "Thank you for obeying the Lord."

Andrew hugged me next and said, "I'm proud of you."

Then woman after woman walked up and shared their stories with me. One by one we cried, hugged, and prayed for one another. These were all miraculous spiritual, mental, and emotional healings, springing up out of love, transparency, vulnerability and obedience.

Over the coming months, both my parents began to find healing from their own experiences of sexual abuse and trauma. Although by then they had been married close to thirty years, they never shared all of their stories with anyone, not even with one another.

I remember when they shared their stories with me for the first time. Finally, they became aware of the shame, guilt, and condemnation they'd lived in for decades. They were now given the keys to unlock the door of their prisons and walk into freedom.

In telling one of my friends, Karen, about this part of my story, we received this revelation: When God spoke to Sister Jay and she declared to me, "Indeed you will," not once but *three* times, God was not only declaring my freedom, He was declaring freedom for both of my parents as well! As God gave us this revelation, we were filled with gratitude, awe, and thanksgiving, and we began to cry and worship God together for His loving, healing power.

April 23, 2011

The day finally arrived. I was closing on my first home! I prayed and cried so much throughout my journey into home ownership. I thanked God for a professional, God-fearing Realtor in Jacque, who had encouraged me through the entire process, including the process of leaving my relationship.

Jacque shared her story with me, and I'm forever grateful. She was a reassuring rock, a tangible representation of how the Lord was with me. I wasn't alone.

After signing the biggest stack of papers I'd ever seen and finalizing all the wires, I held the keys in my hand. I picked up some lunch, turned the key in the door, and walked into my empty home. Sitting in the beautiful, undressed bay window, tears began rolling down my cheeks. Was this really my life? Just eight months ago I was moving out of the apartment I shared with my ex while fighting to keep my life and protect my children's lives—and now I was here. I considered every-thing leading up to this moment. I was grateful, humbled, and hopeful for the future.

Reflecting led me to think of meaningful words my dad had shared with me a few months earlier when I moved out of the apartment I shared with Chance:

"Stephanie, you were at the bottom of a grand staircase. Jesus was at the top of the stairs. Every time you began to ascend, there was a man who would come from behind the staircase and pursue you. They were there to compel you not to continue your ascent up the stairs toward Jesus. Time and time again, over many years you stopped ascending. You would turn back and follow another man. Ultimately, you rejected Jesus' call to come up higher.

Stephanie, I assure you this time is going to be different! If you choose to answer Jesus' persistent, loving call to take the journey up the stairway, you will come to know him, And once at the top of the staircase, you're going to meet a man who is worthy of you."

Because He First Loved Me

Jesus took all the risk by loving me before I even knew how to love Him back. I came to love the Lord because He first loved me (1 John 4:19). Once I began to understand love in Jesus Christ, I stopped lying to myself and pretending I knew how to love others on my own. Through His example, I sought in humility to know and display real love.

Jesus never once said anything to manipulate, take from, deceive, or control me. He loved me despite my doing everything wrong (Romans 5:8). He still protected me and pursued me (Hebrews 13:6). He kept my children and me safe even when I didn't respect Him and didn't follow my parents' instruction.

Even though I enjoyed some real experiences with Jesus when I was younger, I turned my back on Him because the desires of my heart lead me astray (James 1:14). Yet even when I was in trouble, He was still rooting for me, he knew me, saw me, and gave me new mercies every morning (Jeremiah 29:11; Psalm 139:3; Lamentations 3:22–23). He was still praying and singing over me (Romans 8:34; Zephaniah 3:17). He still knew every hair on my head (Psalm 139:2).

Jesus suffered with me through my insecurities, low self-esteem, abuse, anger, abortion, bitterness, unforgiveness, disobedience, unfaithfulness, and pride. He believed in who He made me to be before I ever knew who I was, or what my purpose was.

Jesus was kind to me. He patiently waited on me through my wrong mindsets and behaviors and still blessed me with a loving family and friends. He showed generosity toward me in my jobs even when I made mistakes. He wasn't envious of me. He was the truest gentleman, letting me choose my own way and my own path. And when I chose paths that weren't His choice for me, He still loved me.

When I took the qualities, attributes, and possessions He gave me and chose to serve my idols, He didn't take His gifts from me. He wasn't boastful or loud about how He could condemn or hurt me because I moved in with my fiancé. Instead, He stood patiently at the door of my heart and knocked. He wasn't obligated to, yet He did. And even though He is above me, He didn't treat me less than Himself. Instead, He helped me to see I was made in His image, and I could choose to be like Him. He showed me I was royalty. And even when I wasn't living up to my name, He revealed to me that crowns are a symbol of honor and shouldn't be misused or trampled upon.

When He spoke words of healing over me through my brother Jonathan, He wasn't rude. Instead, He restored my soul and led me back to the place of righteousness (Psalms 23:3). Jesus wasn't looking to use me up selfishly. When I chose to be selfish and fulfill my own needs and desires, leaving me more broken and in the depths of lust, He still sought to give me Himself, to give me living water that would never run dry (John 4:14).

He didn't demand that I change.

Instead, He showed me what I needed to change if I wanted to experience true love.

When I was lost, He didn't use his disappointment, hurt, or anger to hurt me. Instead, He protected me when I lay on the floor in the bathroom of my apartment, fearing for my life. When He could've been vengeful, He covered me. Regardless of all the wrong I've done, He died on the cross for my sins so I wouldn't be indebted with my life. He gave me an abundant life presently and in eternity (John 10:10) even though I took a life.

When I didn't listen, He covered my heart until I was ready to receive the truth. Jesus exposed the lies my heart believed, and He was willing to reveal the truth to me so I could be free (John 8:32). He didn't leave me; He believed and trusted in the fact that He began a good work in me, and He would be faithful to complete it.

Jesus made me a crown and crowned me with His unconditional love. He did these things for me and he is willing to do these things and so much more for you as well.

All you have to do is receive it.

Love was my greatest conquest. I thought love was an ideal. I didn't know it was a person: Jesus Christ.

This is why I know: He is patient and kind. He doesn't envy or boast, and He isn't arrogant. He isn't rude or self-seeking. He isn't easily angered, and He keeps no record of wrong; instead, He rejoices in the truth. He always protects, trusts, hopes, and He never fails (1 Corinthians 13).

An Open Letter to My Daughter Kadiri

I felt led to write a letter to my daughter, which is filled with the most important lessons I have learned through my experiences in becoming a young woman and searching for love. My hope is that others can benefit from these words too.

Kadiri,

I love you. You and Eli'el are the main reason I chose to become the woman I am today, and why I have the courage to keep being refined into a better version of myself each and every year. When you were a baby, you looked exactly like me. Some hopes I have for you were for you not to experience all the abuses I experienced and to eliminate as much hurt and pain from coming into your life as I could. I failed in some areas and succeeded in others.

I'm proud of you. You seek to know Jesus, you apologize when you're wrong, and you make the adjustments you need to. You're a fighter. You have courage. You are caring, fun, and social, and all these are wonderful qualities. When I prayed about how to conclude this book, I heard Jesus speak to my heart to write an open letter to you and to people who need guidance into becoming who Jesus is calling them to become.

When I look at the choices I made growing up, I realized I was searching for love, and I wanted to know how to love others. The thing is, I didn't know what love was. I had a fluid definition of what it was. I was reaching out and trying to grasp it, and it seemed to always slip through my hands.

My search was for someone safe, someone who would know everything about me and accept me despite my past, present, or future mistakes. It wasn't until years later I understood I was looking for someone who would love me unconditionally, a way in which I didn't even love myself.

In my quest for this acceptance, I accepted people I thought I could eventually tell the truth to. People who wouldn't hate me or be disgusted with me, people who would see my remorse and sorrow and assure me that I wasn't evil even though I had done evil things. I wanted to be with someone who believed in second chances.

In other words, I looked for God in men.

The hurt I perpetuated and experienced was all in the name of love, but I wasn't finding or experiencing love at all. In my search, I found out who and what love is, and I want to share what I discovered with you.

LESSON 1

Love Is Patient

Grow Up Faster, Faster, Faster

GROWING UP IS A process. It's an exciting, challenging, difficult, and rewarding journey. It shouldn't be rushed. Did you know everything you can do, you had to learn first? You must be taught everything, and learning takes time.

Impatience followed me into various areas of my life. When I was young, I felt pushed instead of led into relationships. I wanted to find out who I was supposed to be with as soon as possible so I could have a family. I wasn't ready to be married, be a wife, or be a mother.

Instead, my focus should have been on patiently learning who Jesus was through praying, reading, and studying the Bible and being discipled by someone with good fruit in their lives. I needed to learn who I was and what God had called me to do and then go about doing it. This all takes time. Jesus will lead you patiently, and I pray you follow him.

Be patient enough to be taught by the Lord and those he's placed in your life as guides. Ask as many questions as you can. Jesus will bring people into your life who bear good fruit; look around so you will see them.

If you see someone who has a good relationship with the Lord, has good friendships, and is honest, fun, or kind, ask them questions. Then follow the blueprint of how they succeeded in those areas in their lives.

Yes, you are different from other people. However, God set up the world by principles. If you follow the principles, you can learn from others' lives so you, too, will live a blessed life. Some principles I want to share are the importance of gaining knowledge, understanding, and wisdom and what it means to sow and reap. The choices you make will produce good or bad fruit in your life.

In my life you can see how impatient I was and how it caused me a lot of sorrow. I wanted to grow up. I wanted to hurry into adulthood. I wanted to have relational and financial control over my life. I didn't ask enough questions because I thought I was smart and already knew everything. Don't make this mistake. Ask, and be a student of the Lord and wise people who follow His principles in life.

Now I need to tell you about Zion. He was my boyfriend when I was fourteen years old. He was kind, good-natured, inquisitive, respectful, and an intentional young man. Zion's personality was easygoing. One could find him smiling, singing, or dancing. He was a good student, and his aspiration was to be a pilot. We talked on the phone all day long in the summer. We caught the bus to visit one another, often going to the mall, skating, or to church and family functions together. We were inseparable friends and had a beautiful, meaningful relationship. I believed we'd be high school sweethearts, and one day we'd marry.

You can imagine my surprise when I was praying and felt God speaking to my heart to end my relationship with Zion because, "*He's falling in love with you, and he needs to fall in love with Me first.*"

I was devastated; we both were. Everything was going well, plus we believed we were in love. I obeyed God even though what He said made no sense to me. With no guidance on how to keep our friendship or learning who or what love is, we fell apart. In my hurt I became angry and impatient with God.

What I didn't know then was Zion and I were developing a codependent relationship. Codependency would've been detrimental to our overall development as individuals. We didn't know ourselves. We also didn't know God or what love actually was; we were young and lacked guidance. Years later, Zion and I reconnected, and time told the truths I could not see at age fourteen.

In college, I found myself in a triangle with Zion and his ex-girlfriend.

He said things like, "You're amazing. Your wifey material, but I want to see what else is out there."

Second best was the position I played in his life for a while because I wanted to be chosen and accepted. One Valentine's Day, we gave one another small gifts, ate lunch, and went to the movies together. He saw his ex-girlfriend there with her date and sulked the rest of the evening. I was humiliated and chose never to date Zion again.

Unfortunately for Zion, through experiencing the dark side of promiscuity and being misinformed, he aligned himself with doctrines of the occult. Fifteen years later, I knew why God said Zion needed to know and fall in love with Him first. If Zion and I would have found out God is love and how love is exemplified as stated in 1 Corinthians 13, we would've been fulfilled by pure love. This experience would have given us both the opportunity to begin loving ourselves and others well, and possibly even one another.

Purity vs. Virginity

I didn't understand more than priding myself in virginity. I should strive for purity because that is the foundation to the former. What dignity would I achieve and what glory would God get out of me seeing how close I could get to going all the way with the men I dated, but then choosing to abstain? This mentality caused me to continue to have multiple temporary relationships where I eventually regretted my lack of boundaries. Holding hands and kissing quickly escalated into passionate, intimate touches.

Regrettably, I didn't consistently seek out transparent, godly, or practical knowledge on friendships, dating, marriage, or healthy familial relationships. My lack of boundaries when it came to physical intimacy became a stumbling block to what I was actually searching for: love. I wanted to be in a loving, fun relationship where I shared a deep connection with my mate.

Continuing in these compromising practices took me to the point where it was just a matter of time before I lost my virginity. Although my virginity was holding on by a thread, by the time I was seventeen I had already been cheated on a couple of times by young men I dated who didn't share my same values. The first betrayal planted a seed of doubt that I would be able to date someone who valued faithfulness like I did.

The following betrayals reinforced my fear that if I didn't compromise in my standard of marriage before sex, I was going to continue being cheated on. Instead of believing there was something inherently wrong with who I was choosing to date, I believed my standard was too high.

Ultimately, when I was told by Kahlil he didn't see himself continuing on in our abstinent relationship much longer, I chose to compromise. I didn't believe it was as risky as it was because I believed we would get married. Instead, I lost my virginity, I lost my relationship, I lost my trust for people, I lost my option to go to college out of state. As a result, I became an unwed teenage mother.

Virginity is a personal gift you bring to a relationship. Once it is given, you won't ever get it back. In the culture you're growing up in, people don't know who they are, and because of this they devalue themselves. In this distorted mindset, there are people, like me, who make choices that have life-altering consequences. I want to share with you Dinah's story (Genesis 34). Although she was a princess, she didn't know who she was. From her lack of belief in her identity, she made life-altering choices.

Dinah was the thirteenth-born child to Jacob and Leah. Jacob's name was changed by God to Israel, which means *prince.* So not only was Dinah the youngest and only girl, she was a princess too. In the account, Dinah went out to see the daughters of the land. While she was out, it appears she was unprotected by her father or her brothers because a Hivite, or Shechem (a prince of the country she was exploring), took her and slept with her. Scripture said he "defiled Dinah" (v. 5). To defile means to weaken, mishandle, or to afflict.

One of the ways we as women can be defiled is if we do not know who we are. Not knowing who you are sets you up to be abused. It seems Dinah didn't identify with who she was, a princess. I say this because she consensually slept with a man she hadn't married, even though her worth was great. Her conduct proves that although she probably knew premarital sex was wrong, especially in her position, there was a part of her that didn't believe she was worth the position given to her by the Lord.

If a woman doesn't know or believe who she is, she can't occupy the positions Jesus has crowned her to be in. If we as women don't believe who we are, we won't submit to the necessary protection and guidance given to us by Jesus or those He has entrusted us with.

Even celebrities, who aren't royalty, have security teams because they are committed to their well-being and safety. I wonder why Dinah was so irresponsible with her well-being and safety even though she was royalty? She exemplified inappropriate and harmful practices and behaviors in a foreign land.

Like Dinah, many young women can attribute their poor choices to lust. Lust is fueled by our senses. We saw a show, heard a song, watched a movie, read a book, admired someone's beauty, talked to a friend or family member who told us what we needed to know about men, homes, cars, educational status, fashion, children, relationships, church, God, religion, travel, or any other plethora of information. And yes, some of it was true. I would say a majority was a lie wrapped in fragments of the truth. What is deceitful about lust is that, in many cases, the things we desire aren't evil.

1 Peter 2:9 says, "But ye are a chosen generation, a royal priesthood, a holy nation, a peculiar people; that ye should shew forth the praises of him who hath called you out of darkness into his marvelous light." Do you see? Just as Dinah was royalty, we are too. But will we be like her, not fully accepting our position by protecting it? Or will we choose to be lead astray by our own desires, even the good ones?

Fornication

Further in 1 Corinthians

> Now the body *is* not for sexual immorality but for the Lord, and the Lord for the body. Or do you not know

206

that he who is joined to a harlot is one body with her? For "the two," He says, "shall become one flesh." But he who is joined to the Lord is one spirit with Him. Flee sexual immorality. Every sin that a man does is outside the body, but he who commits sexual immorality sins against his own body. Or do you not know that your body is the temple of the Holy Spirit who is in you, whom you have from God, and you are not your own? For you were bought at a price; therefore glorify God in your body and in your spirit, which are God's.

Kadiri, let's talk about the revelation I received from the above passage. As a woman, I prided myself in being faithful to the men I was in a relationship with. Naturally, I was devastated when I learned men I'd been faithful to weren't faithful to me. Through the healing process, I realized I had done to God what men had done to me. When I chose to be baptized in Jesus' name and receive the infilling of the Holy Ghost and spoke in a heavenly language, I had become the bride of Christ. Although I was His bride, I didn't keep my vows through obedience to the biblical standard for sex only in marriage.

Jesus showed me I was so valuable to Him that He committed all He had to me. He laid down His life so that I may have life and have it more abundantly. Until a man and I are willing to forsake all others and commit our lives to one another, our relationship isn't stable or special enough to share the gift of sex with one another. Women who become wives are admonished to listen to and respect their husbands. I've found it is a lot easier to listen to and respect someone who truly loves you and has your best interests at heart. The healthy relationship I desired to have with a man would first need to be established in my relationship with the Lord through obedience.

Grandma Risa said she gained a lot of respect for Grandpa Eric because he was abstinent for four years prior to dating her, and they continued abstinence until they were married. She witnessed in him a fruit of the spirit: self-control. It's important individuals learn self-control in their singleness because if they want to be married, self-control is a virtue they will need to stay committed and to endure hardships that arise in the relationship.

The Lord tells men and women that fornication is a sin against our own bodies. Jesus also tells men in particular to love their wives as their own bodies. If you meet a single man who is a fornicator, at that point in their journey, that man wouldn't be a godly future husband. First, because they lack self-control. Second, they are sinning against their own body, which shows a lack of love for themselves.

We should love others as we love ourselves. If a man doesn't love himself, he doesn't have the ability to love you; not because he doesn't want to; it's because he isn't able to give something he doesn't possess within his heart for himself. Ask yourself, "Does the man I'm interested in exemplify the characteristics of 1 Corinthians 13 towards himself?" That's a principle of the kingdom, to love Jesus, to love yourself, and then to love your neighbor as you love yourself. When the Lord helps a single person develop an authentic love through relationship with Him and others, I've found they have a greater capacity to love their spouse in the future.

Jesus tells men it's also their responsibility to love their wives as He loves the church and gave Himself for it. Ways in which we give of ourselves to others is spiritually, relationally, mentally, emotionally, physically, and financially. Sadly, as a culture we quickly give ourselves to one another physically while simultaneously stealing true intimacy from one another in all the other areas I mentioned above.

We say we're giving all of ourselves, yet really we're holding back our truest selves. We then wonder why our relationships have no substance. In reality, we sleep with people we don't know. In time, our character is exposed through the storms of life, and when we have no anchor in intimacy with Jesus, ourselves, and those closest to us, we become shipwrecked. Being stuck, tattered, and broken up by life's storms deeply impacts our lives.

At the end of the day, your purity and your virginity is yours. You decide how to use it. Don't feel pressured into having sex or doing physically intimate things with someone you don't know and who doesn't know you, and someone who is not committed to you in marriage. As people made in the image of God, we are all worthy of being known. Kadiri, you are royalty, so set the standard; you don't have to do what everyone else is doing. Your decisions in this area of your life have lasting effects, either good or bad. Sex is powerful, it's fun, and it's connecting and has the ability to create life; I can guarantee you the best way to experience this is in a committed, loving marriage.

Ultimately, my hope and prayer for you, Lady Bug, is that you share the gift of you with a man who loves God, loves himself, and loves you. Men made extravagant promises to me. I wish I'd waited to witness their actions before giving myself to men who didn't love me or know me. I hope you wait on the relationship where you both seek to know God, yourselves and one another intimately. The legacy Grandma Risa established for you and me was a heritage of waiting and marriage. And if you choose, you can restore and carry on the legacy.

LESSON 2

Love Is Kind

Caught off Guard

KADIRI, IF SOMEONE TOLD me in my early teens I would be in abusive relationships from ages sixteen to twenty-four, I would've never believed them. I would've told them they were surely mistaken. I knew the difference between good men and bad ones. I didn't want to be with the bad boy; nothing about their lifestyle or mentality was appealing to me. I thought I was too mature and too smart to make that mistake.

I saw firsthand a family member and their spouse fighting with brooms in a small kitchen when I was a child. It made me feel so afraid. I visited cousins in the hospital after they'd encountered domestic disputes. I disliked arguments and dreaded witnessing an anger that would cause fights between people who were supposed to treasure one another. It was infuriating seeing my pregnant loved one with a black eye.

So you can imagine how confusing it was to be treated poorly by someone who was supposed to protect me. Soon enough, the mistreatment made me into an unrecognizable person. Unkindness smothered my light. As much as it made me angry, it made me timid and afraid. Unkindness bruised my self-esteem in ways I struggle to articulate even now.

Growing Up with a Gentleman

It was difficult for me to find the words to describe what I was experiencing in my romantic relationships. How I was treated was the opposite of what I witnessed in my household growing up with my mother and father. What I experienced was verbal, mental, emotional, and physical abuse. I grew up in a home with your grandpa Murray, a faithful, respectful, hardworking, and caring gentleman. Your grandma Risa wanted to marry a gentleman. I'm glad she received her heart's desire.

Your grandpa Murray emphasized to my brothers and me respecting, caring for, and loving one another. When we were kids, he told us he and our mom wouldn't always be alive. Your grandparents didn't allow us to practice mistreating one another. We did mistreat one another, but it was always corrected when your grandparents heard it or saw it. I was naïve in believing the men I dated grew up like me and received the same values. When men mistreated me at first, I remember being in shock. I had never witnessed my mom being treated this way.

I always felt like their behavior was unwarranted. My compassion told me to give people a second chance; everyone makes mistakes. I knew I wanted to be forgiven for the mistakes I'd made, so I often got angry and believed I forgave quickly. By nature, I'm a peacemaker and conflict adverse. In conflict I'm uncomfortable, so I would say I forgave in order to get out of feeling uncomfortable, not because I'd forgiven. I did this to my detriment. There are times when Jesus will call you to forgive and reconcile and there are times, he will call you to forgive and disconnect from people, places, or situations detrimental to you.

No Criteria

Growing up I hadn't witnessed my parents cussing, cheating, demeaning, or disrespecting each other. They were poor at communicating at times, yet when they did communicate, it wasn't the abuse I was exposed to early on in my romantic relationships. Back then, I often deceived myself into believing someone felt bad about abusing me. For instance, when someone called me out of my name, cursed at me, pushed, held, accused, or threatened me, I assumed they felt bad about their actions.

I thought this because I knew if I ever did those things to them, I would be remorseful. I believed the men I dated had hearts like mine. Inside, I somehow felt I would easily find empathy because I was empathetic. I believed I had the ability to reason with whomever I was dating; regrettably, I was so emotional they couldn't hear me. Some refused to hear me.

I later learned love has standards and holds people accountable for their actions because love rejoices in truth. You can like someone and even love them, but if they aren't kind to you, then they don't love you, no matter what they say. You will know people by their actions more than by their words. Scripture says you will know them by their fruit (Matthew 7:20). Ask yourself, "What is the fruit of the people in my life?" We must forgive, yet when people have a pattern of being unkind, and an unwillingness to change, Jesus can lead you to exit their life. Unkindness will wound your vibrant spirit.

Lesson 3

Love Doesn't Envy or Boast and Is Not Arrogant

Becoming Enemies

I NEVER CONSIDERED WHAT would happen if the man I was dating became my enemy instead of remaining my lover and friend. When it happened, it felt sudden. Truly, the progression was gradual. I would say it began when the men I was dating became unhappy with their own lives. This discontentment turned into comparison. Oftentimes, comparison begins in our minds first before we ever utter words or walk it out in our actions. We may wonder why someone has something we want or can do something we want to do. It may begin as admiration, yet if we think them having it is unfair, then those thoughts can lead us into believing they don't deserve it. Then we criticize them because of our envy.

My definition of *envy* is an overwhelming feeling of discontentment, a resentful longing, hatred, or anger toward someone because of a desire to have the qualities, attributes, or possessions of another without regard of the rights of that person. I don't believe the men I was in relationship with consciously knew envy was behind why they thought and felt differently about me; however, their actions soon followed their thoughts and feelings toward me. For many years I never understood why I was so discouraged, accused, and demeaned by the men I loved and who said they loved me. I now know it was because of envy.

It's strange when a fight ensues silently at first. Then discontentment increases, and a person's words and actions eventually erupt. When I began relationships, there was an unspoken expectation that we would always be on the same team. We would look out for one another and build something together that would be ours. I believed we would give it our all because we cared about prospering our life together.

It wasn't until years later I realized I had this expectation based on what I'd seen my parents do in their marriage. Even though I wasn't in a covenant relationship, I expected the benefits of one. Pay attention, Kadiri, if a man's admiration of you changes into a scowl, or cutting, mean, and critical words. When you are being celebrated, are they the loudest one cheering? Are they encouraging you? Do they acknowledge your accomplishments? Are they willing to pray for you and help you grow? These are all important questions to ask yourself about who you choose to do life with.

Nothing Is Free

On various occasions, different men I dated tried to control my actions by what they had, or by their abilities. At times kindnesses were snatched back because I didn't perform in the ways they expected me to. Nothing was freely given. Other times, men would use their strength not to protect me; they used it to intimidate or hurt me. They would boast about what they possessed, what they could do, or who they were. The excessiveness of it would be sickening to hear over time.

I hated to hear how they thought of other people because they would be so condescending. At times I was so shocked I wondered how we were even together, or what I even liked about them. I even wondered, *Do they really love me or care about me?*

I've always felt extremely uncomfortable talking about myself. Which is another reason why I struggled so much to write this book. If people found out I'd done something, it was because they asked or they found out, not because I shared it with them initially. I would play small, shrink myself, and try to be status quo in order not to get attention, good or bad.

I lived in constant fear of not being good enough. My greatest desire was to help my family. We'd suffered a lot, and I didn't want us to suffer anymore. I worked hard for my family. I only strived to use my good for others. This truth isn't shared to elevate my morality just for you to understand how hurt I was and how I didn't understand why men I loved used their good against me instead of for me.

Subconsciously, I knew it was only a matter of time before their sentiments of me would change. It took time to see these parts of their character. Character is the foundation of every person. It is something not seen initially and is discovered over time. Life's triumphs and trials expose our character to ourselves and to anyone else who witnesses our lives.

Over the years, I've seen how any relationship, couple, or marriage is only as strong as those individuals who make up the relationship. The Bible calls character the "hidden man of the heart" (I Peter 3:4). Life's troubles and hardships exposed the *hidden man of my heart* and the heart of the men I loved.

I'm Better Than You

For someone with low self-esteem, Kadiri, I was surprised to find out I was self-righteous. I thought the good I'd done was because I was a good person, not because of my connection with God or him allowing my parents to teach me some good values and allowed me to follow some of those values well. I felt so low about myself, so I found satisfaction in comparing any morality I had to those around me, including my romantic partners.

I didn't act this way constantly, but often enough for me to become arrogant over time. At the end of the day, I thought I was morally superior to them. My arrogance was a wall I built to elevate and protect myself from the criticisms and opinions of others, especially them. It didn't work. Those beliefs and mindsets were the foundation of my low self-esteem, and it was like sinking sand.

I knew me, and I wasn't happy with me. I held secrets. Deep down inside I didn't believe I was worthy of God's forgiveness, or the forgiveness of those I'd hurt, so I didn't forgive myself either. Once I became transparent and began confessing my faults, I was able to receive God's forgiveness, the forgiveness of others, and even the forgiveness of myself. Now, when I want to elevate my sense of morality over others in order to feel good about myself, I realize there must be a deep place in my heart of hidden sin that needs to be confessed and healed.

I began to seek healing from God in those areas. I sought to receive understanding, compassion, grace, mercy, forgiveness, and love from God so I could turn away from my sins and sincerely love myself. Even still, I have to intentionally ask God for help to practice these things. It's the only way I can replace my self-righteous arrogance with all the beautiful gifts God has freely given to me. He says, "Freely you have received, freely give" (Matthew 10:8).

LESSON 4

Love Isn't Rude or Selfish

Bit by Puppy Love

KADIRI, MY HEART TRULY goes out to people who have grown up and engaged in dysfunctional relationships. I have met multiple women who have known and grown up with lovers-turned-abusers, and they have a true bond. They have known them so long they became their first everything. The first person they kissed, slept with, moved into an apartment with, bought a home with, married, and had children with.

They trusted them fully because they were their friends first. Sure, looking back there were red flags, but most thirteen-year-olds haven't lived long enough to know what to look for. Feelings and emotions are what guide most young girls and boys. This is a precarious position to be in, trying to establish a relationship with someone on the outside while one's focus should be to establish a relationship with God and within oneself first.

Even in algebraic formulas there is an order of operation. Do you remember the acronym PEMDAS? If you solved a problem in this order, then the likelihood of solving the equation was certain if your calculations were correct. If one didn't follow the order of operations, there was nearly no chance a person would come up with the right answer unless they randomly chose the correct answer.

When we seek relationships out of order, we essentially gamble our heart and the hearts of others. Before fully developing personal understanding, we begin trying to establish a relationship with others out of loneliness. Years lived is what it costs to know God, oneself, and to even have the hope of knowing another person. I was too young to be dating. I hadn't developed the spiritual, mental, emotional, and relational roots I needed to bear the fruit of a healthy relationship. Not knowing God or myself caused me to engage in relationships prematurely that became abusive over time.

I would encourage you to always start by being a man's friend. An actual friend, not friends with benefits; we'll, talk about that next. It's important to be a man's friend because friendships usually are based on common interests outside of yourselves. In common interests you both begin to realize who the other person is authentically. I wasn't good at establishing solid friendships before romance with the men I chose to date.

Through friendship you see how people live, what's important to them, and who influences their life. You see how they deal with stress and how they work. You learn about their dreams and their family, and you get to see how they treat people. That's an invaluable experience to have.

If I followed the order of operations in relationships, I would have seen how rude some of the men I dated were. How they handled conflict or mistreatment was honestly embarrassing. They didn't have emotional stability. They were rude, cutting, and disrespectful.

How a man treats someone he perceives he doesn't need, or how he treats a person who has wronged him knowingly or unknowingly is telling of his character. Pay close attention to these things because in any relationship, grievances come up, and he will treat you how he treats others who have wronged him.

Over Waiting

From time to time when I became an adult, I found myself missing Sean, a boy I dated from church when I was a teenager. I hadn't spoken to him in years; however, I had good memories with him, and I liked his family. I saw him on Facebook over ten years later, and we began to talk. Later during the week we met up to have dinner and catch up. He was the same and different. We had a lot to talk about and shared a lot of similar experiences. He was easy to talk to. We laughed a lot, gave each other advice, saw movies, and visited restaurants from time to time. We were beginning to become friends.

My last breakup almost took my mind and my life, so I decided I needed to approach relationships differently. I talked to and went out on dates with different people periodically, yet I hadn't gotten this close to anyone previously. To be honest, the first few years of my singleness I had no interest in being in a relationship. After I experienced more healing within myself, I began desiring to be in a godly, loving, fun relationship. I still hoped to get married one day.

One night we were on the phone, and something he said shocked me. He articulated who he knew me to be at my core. It made me cry because although I had you and Eli'el with your fathers, neither one of them truly knew me.

I never told Sean that what he'd said impacted me. It scared me, and I wondered why he saw me the way he did and how he knew what he knew about me. I didn't feel we had the conversations needed to reveal those truths. Nonetheless, he knew.

We continued to become friends until we kissed. Soon after we crossed the physical boundaries of our relationship, everything became awkward; nothing was the same and we never talked about it. Prior to becoming physical, we could talk for hours and relate on most things. We talked about the risks of crossing our friendship boundary, yet we took a chance anyway. I wish we hadn't. He was newly divorced and single for less time than me. He was still trying to figure out what he wanted. I should've been a better friend. Instead, I began thinking more about myself than him. Pastor Marquies says the fruit of selfishness is death. Once again, my selfishness began the death of our relationship.

LESSON 5

Love Isn't Easily Angered and Keeps No Record of Wrong

Cycles

AS YOU READ THE book, could you see the bad cycles I walked out in my relationships? Over time, the cycles I walked in increasingly got worse and worse. One destructive cycle I found myself in was one of anger that was fueled by intimidation and caused me to become fearful, unforgiving, and bitter. Everyone gets angry; anger is an emotion that God gave us. At times even God gets angry; however, what the Bible instructs us to do is to be angry and don't sin. That's difficult to do without God's help.

It takes a lot for me to get angry, yet in my relationships I slowly became angrier and angrier faster and faster. At times I was furious. Those negative emotions and feelings made me feel physically sick at times. When I threw a vase in my room and put a hole in my wall, I didn't even recognize myself. In healthy relationships people still get angry, the difference is they have self-control in the midst of their anger.

Self-Control

When someone has self-control, they won't seek to hurt the other person physically or verbally. Instead, they'll speak the truth in love. Don't demean, call people names, or use intimidation and embarrassment to make people feel low. I caution you to never emotionally hurt the people you love when you get angry. Ignoring someone, not speaking to someone, or leaving for days at a time without communicating is all emotional abuse. It's okay to take a break in a heated argument to collect your thoughts. Go for a walk, pray, and calm down.

Words given and actions taken in anger aren't soon forgotten and have lasting effects. When a person gets angry and doesn't have any self-control, it's a sign the relationship isn't going to last if they don't change. Instead, when you have a disagreement, seek to understand the other person. It's equally important to take the time needed to assist the other person in understanding you as well.

Different men I dated became so fierce with their words and actions, it caused me to feel intimidated and fearful of them. Soon, I no longer trusted them. With each passing explosion of anger and disrespect, the hurt I felt deepened. It never seemed like their apologies and subsequent actions allowed me to heal, and I became unforgiving. By the end of the relationship, my hurt, fear ,and anger turned to hatred and bitterness. My heart was hardened, and I built up walls to protect myself. My walls could be erected in moments, especially with new people I met. If I saw any inclination of character flaws that hurt me in the past, I disengaged as soon as I could.

I kept a record of every wrong. I felt weighed down by the heaviness of unforgiveness, hatred, and fear. It takes a lot of mental and emotional space to hold onto these emotions instead of facing and releasing them. In this condition it was impossible to fully receive or give God's love. When I chose to stop keeping record of wrongs and judging others and myself for who we were at our worst, then I was able to experience the love of God. God's love healed me. This is a continual process. I fight to keep my heart pure in spite of hurt I still experience from time to time.

My friend Tim said, "There's no hurt deeper than God can heal you."

I choose to believe this. It gives me abundant hope and resolve to forgive so I can be forgiven, free, and happy.

LESSON 6

Love Rejoices in the Truth

I Can Fix Him

MANY YEARS AGO, GRANDPA Murray told me about a vision he'd had. In his vision, he saw a woman who was faithful to God and faithful in serving others in the house of God.

After a while, the vision switched and he saw this same woman leave the church, go into the street, and find a man. She picked that man up and dragged him into the church.

The astounding part of this vision was that the man the woman dragged into the church was dead. She drug his dead corpse in, lifted it up onto a seat, and straightened his back so he wouldn't fall, then sat next to him.

Although your grandfather didn't have this vision about me, this was exactly what I did.

Missionary Dating

Recently, I've heard a term some use to describe this faulty practice. They call it "missionary dating." In essence, it means dating someone who doesn't serve the Lord while you declare your intention of serving the Lord. In this intention to serve the Lord, women and men may find themselves lonely and single. These feelings and emotions must be managed, and few people know how to do so. Instead, their soul begins to search. They go out from the presence of the Lord, searching for connection. An intricate trap is set for individuals whose souls begin to search; although they were physically sitting in and some are even serving in the church.

Driving desires lead us all. For me, I felt a deep sense of lack, and it drove me. My drive was insatiable and would stop at nothing. I was no longer led by the spirit of love I was led by lust. Lust justifies the consumption of another's well-being in order to be fulfilled. In this state of mind, even the kindest person's intentions can't be trusted.

Love causes us to give and serve from the abundance of love we have received from the unconditional love of Christ. In love, I've found the attitude displayed is often, *how can I help you?* Not rescue or fix, just how can I assist you from who I am and what I have been given from the love of Christ. Only Jesus can rescue and fix people, not us.

Those intentions will cause a godly woman to meet a man and start by sharing with them the most important relationship in their life, their relationship with Jesus. The disingenuous action of backtracking and trying to be a witness after I compromised in my pursuit of the relationship and my willingness to be entertained by various unsaved men exposed the true intentions of my heart.

See, the relationship was never about honoring the Lord or giving to the other person in relationship with me the life-changing experience I'd experienced in knowing God. It was about me. It was about them fulfilling my need for companionship. Relationships that begin on this premise usually don't last. The few that do must first be torn down to the foundation and rebuilt on their joint belief and faith in Jesus. Over the years I have found if a couple's foundation isn't the same in the area of faith, they have different views of life and how it should be lived. Often these views are so opposite there is no way to sustain a lasting relationship.

LESSON 7

Love Always Protects, Trusts, Hopes, and Never Fails

Unsafe

FEAR SET IN WHEN abuse entered my relationships. I didn't feel protected. Abuse is about maintaining control of others so the abuser feels in control of their own life. They do this by using other people to fulfill their own personal desires. It's an act of selfishness and self-preservation. I have realized a common thread between people who become abusive. They are traumatized, aimless, fearful, selfish, and insecure people. Scripture urges us to love our neighbor as we love ourselves. Whenever a person mistreats someone, it is a clear indication of the person's lack of self-love.

Myles Munroe, a powerful evangelist, author, and speaker, said, "When purpose is unknown, abuse is inevitable." Kadiri, this is why knowing your purpose is so important. I can now see a clear correlation between the deterioration of vision and purpose and how it impacted the men I dated. Over time, this deterioration affected how they treated everyone around them, including themselves.

I hope you will go on the journey to find out what your purpose is so you will become who God had in mind when He created you. Seeking God to know your purpose is a special journey. Once you find your purpose, I pray you appreciate and value it. Valuing your own purpose will help you value others' purposes as well. You will begin to understand why it is so important to protect and to be protected in relationships. Once you see the greatness living on the inside of you and others, you realize what it means to be made in the image of God.

A Hopeful Trust

When we enter into a relationship, there is a hope that it will last. Relationships carry weight though. At times the weight is so heavy that neither person can sustain it. When you or someone you're in relationship with falls, you will want Jesus to be your foundation, the One you both have your hope and trust in. At different times in your journey, either one or both of you will need to free-fall into Jesus' arms. I did not have assurance in my relationships. Instead, I hoped everything would be okay, and I trusted in the other person and in myself.

Trust is one cornerstone of any healthy relationship. Trust was consistently broken in various ways throughout my relationships. We lost trust in one another when our expectations of one another weren't communicated and therefore not met. It takes courage to be vulnerable enough to tell a person what you expect, or what makes you sad when they hurt you. When promises aren't kept and actions don't match our words, the relationship is set for destruction because the foundation was never based in the love of Jesus.

I'm five two. Can you imagine me holding a grown man up above my head for an extended amount of time? The idea is absurd at best. Even though I would never attempt this feat physically, I tried to do it spiritually. Through my own efforts, I tried to present or dedicate men to God like parents do with their infant children. The problem is, I tried to determine their salvation with controlling prayers to ultimately benefit our relationship, not the man's relationship with Jesus.

Everyone has his or her own will. Most the men I engaged with didn't decide to hold themselves up or present themselves before the Lord, and neither had I. We weren't humble enough to admit neither of our standards of living pleased the Lord. We believed our way was right, and where it wasn't right it would still work out, eventually. I believed it would just take some more time.

What I found was that my indiscretions and compromises only increased; they didn't subside like I would've hoped. In Proverbs 21:2 it says, "Every way of a man is right in his own eyes: but the LORD pondereth the hearts" (KJV). Only in humility can one present themselves to the Lord and appreciate their need of a savior who loved them first.

Failure

Knowing the truth about lust and love helped me understand why every one of my previous relationships failed. Underlining desires, insecurities, and fears gave way to lust. I lacked real love, and so did they. We didn't choose to consistently show kindness, patience, and celebration; instead, we walked in envy and pride. We practiced being rude, angry, and selfish. We refused to consistently change and forgive. Our relationships weren't founded on truth, so we didn't cover one another. We failed to put our full trust and hope in Jesus; instead, we trusted one another and ourselves. Failure was inevitable.

In lust I tried to get an imperfect person to fulfill my needs, desires, wants, and voids. I was searching for love while operating out of lust. I thought I needed to be with someone in order to feel fulfilled; to have companionship, happiness, and purpose; and to be validated. All I ever experienced in my romantic relationships was the consumption of one another not giving love to one another. As I operated in lust, I attracted men who operated in lust too. We took from one another until there was nothing left. This is the opposite of love.

Love

Love is giving and sustaining; it's not selfish. It's about adding love to another person out of the abundance of the love you have received from the Lord. In a relationship like this, no one has to use the other person because they are already fulfilled and overflowing in love. None of my relationships were based on unconditional love; eventually, we no longer had anything to give or take, so we abandoned one another. But we didn't just leave; we left the other person worse off than when we first connected.

It's been a journey learning how to love unconditionally. Every year I seek to become more unconditional in my love for people. Whether it be a loved one or an enemy. This desire has come with a lot of pain in the relationships closest to me. It has stretched me to exemplify the truths in 1 Corinthians 13. What makes unconditional love pure is giving it freely to all those around me without expecting anything in return from them. Instead, I look to God to fulfil me when I feel I lack the love I need.

See, love is a seed. Sow it everywhere you go. Sometimes it will fall on good ground, and you'll witness an abundance of love from the those you loved. Sometimes you will sow love and you won't receive it back from the person or place you sowed it. Yet God promises that you will reap what you sow (Galatians 6:7). "And let us not be weary in well doing: for in due season we shall reap, if we faint not" (Galatians 6:9). What makes it unconditional is you not expecting love from the person God allowed you to show love to. Instead, be kind, even if they aren't. Don't keep a record of wrong, even if others are unforgiving. Celebrate others, even if they are envious toward you. Do exactly what God instructs you to do in each relationship you are in. Nothing more and nothing less. He will give you the discernment to know who you should connect to or not and how to navigate the relationship so you're not abused or abusing others. In essence it's like Uncle Jonathan said in his latest message: "Fear no evil. God is with you."

I'm going to end this chapter by telling you what happened after my relationship with Sean became physical. Almost immediately, he became uncommunicative with me. Once again, all the horrible feelings of not being enough flooded me. But why? Why were my desires continually disappointed? When would I be chosen? As I sat and thought about the situation, all the statements of rejection I heard from various men I had dated flooded back.

One man told me I was wifey material, but he needed to see who else was out there. Another man told me I was a good catch; he just wasn't the bait. That one made me laugh. One of the most hurtful experiences I had was when I found out I was pregnant, and Kahlil told me he was dating someone else. A different time, I was rejected because of my passion for truth and worship, and the fact I'd received the Holy Spirit and spoke in tongues.

Why was I always let down even when I put my best foot forward? These were the questions I had when Jonathan attempted suicide. The relationship I had with Sean felt strained, so I waited a week to let him know what had happened with Jonathan.

When I talked to Sean, he was empathetic, and I appreciated having someone to talk to. Those in our family I could usually talk to were all in crisis mode, too, which made it difficult to process the situation. Sean said he'd check in with me later. The only thing is, he never did.

Countless times I pulled up his name to call or text him; however, deep down in my spirit I knew I shouldn't, so I resisted the urge to reach out. I began to realize that this wasn't a time to lie to myself. The truth was Sean didn't reach out because he didn't want to. Me calling him wouldn't be fair and would put him in a position he didn't want to be in.

So I just kept crying out to Jesus. I won't lie and say I wouldn't have appreciated someone with whom I could vent and process information with. Someone on the outside of the situation who could bring me strength and stability. I consciously worked not to make him my strength, my idol, or my anesthesia to numb the pain. Instead, I bore the pain. When I prayed, I often found myself telling the Lord, "I'm sorry, but I want to call Sean. I don't really want to pray right now."

Yet while in prayer, I began to embrace the pain and allow it to teach me. Previously, I believed I was completely secure in Jesus. I found out I wasn't secure in Him in my pain. Being in abusive relationships caused me to fear all pain. I didn't grasp purposeful, growth-inducing pain. And now, through Jesus' love and grace, I do. See, in pain or ease we are called to abide or stay in the vine whose Christ (John 15:4-9). This is the only way we can have the fruit of his Spirit described in (Galatians 5:22-23), including unconditional love. Without him we can do none of these things. When we are connected with him, we produce his fruit, love, joy, peace, long suffering, gentleness, goodness, faith, meekness, and temperance. Remember when God gave Sister Brooke a revelation about the word charity being used in the KJV version of 1 Corinthians 13 instead of the word love and how when someone gives charity they are not looking for anything in return? This is the kind of love God is desiring to display through all his people.

Pain taught me Jesus is my only constant. It taught me sometimes He will give me someone to endure pain with. They are a gift from Him, and I'm eternally grateful to Him for their steadfastness. Jesus is the only one who truly knows me—past, present, and future. He knows exactly how I feel, and still loves me. Jesus will never leave me physically, and He'll never forsake me emotionally. He is more than enough. He is unconditional love, and he never fails, Kadiri—never.

Acknowledgements

I AM SO GRATEFUL for the compassion, patience, and providence the Lord gave to me throughout this journey.

I want to thank my parents and brothers for allowing me to use Matthew's gift to bring this book to fruition, and for encouraging me along our lives journey together.

I am also indebted to my family and friends who exemplified love to me when I questioned whether I knew what love was, or if I even deserved it. Thank you for loving me. Your love, prayers, and deeds saved my life.

Finally, I want to thank the entire Illumify team and President Mike Klassen, as well as coach Karen Bouchard for your guidance, support, and expertise.

About the Author

STEPHANIE MURRAY IS A believer and follower of Jesus Christ, the mother of two incredible children, the one and only daughter of her loving parents, and sister to 4 amazing brothers. Stephanie is abundantly blessed to be a friend, support and confidant to many. She enjoys teaching, coaching, being outdoors, gardening, traveling, reading, deep conversations, and laughing. One of the greatest gifts of her life is to have connected, genuine and loving relationships in every area of her life.

Stephanie graduated from the University of Colorado at Denver in Sociology and Business. She is the founder of Journey to Your Haven, a nonprofit that serves abused women and their children. For Stephanie, being a part of the transformation of lives from the inside out is truly a calling, honor, and privilege.

To learn about having Stephanie speak at your church or organization, email s.lavonnem@gmail.com.

www.ingramcontent.com/pod-product-compliance
Lightning Source LLC
Chambersburg PA
CBHW031457120626
46545CB00005B/1642